THE RED WINGS

Also by Brian McFarlane

It Happened in Hockey

More It Happened in Hockey

Still More It Happened in Hockey

The Best of It Happened in Hockey

Stanley Cup Fever

Proud Past, Bright Future

It Happened in Baseball

The Leafs

The Habs

The Rangers

THE RED WINGS

BRIAN
MCFARLANE'S
ORIGINAL
SIX

BRIAN MCFARLANE

Published in 1998 by Stoddart Publishing Co. Limited
34 Lesmill Road, Toronto, Canada M3B 2T6

Distributed in Canada by General Distribution Services Limited
325 Humber College Blvd., Toronto, Ontario M9W 7C3
Tel. (416) 213-1919   Fax (416) 213-1917
Email Customer.Service@ccmailgw.genpub.com

Distributed in the U.S. by General Distribution Services Inc.
85 River Rock Drive, Suite 202, Buffalo, New York 14207
Toll-free tel. 1-800-805-1083 Toll-free fax 1-800-481-6207
Email gdsinc@genpub.com

01 00 99 98 1 2 3 4 5

Cataloguing in Publication Data

McFarlane, Brian, 1931–
The Red Wings

(Brian McFarlane's original six)

ISBN 0-7737-3116-4

1. Detroit Red Wings (Hockey team) – History – Anecdotes.
I. Title.   II. Series: McFarlane, Brian, 1931–   .
Brian McFarlane's original six.

GV848.D4M33 1998   796.962'
64' 0977434   C98-931487-1

Every reasonable effort has been made to obtain reprint permissions.
The publisher will gladly receive any information that will help
rectify, in subsequent editions, any inadvertent omissions.

Cover design: Bill Douglas @ The Bang
Cover photo: Hockey Hall of Fame
Design and typesetting: Kinetics Design & Illustration

Printed and bound in Canada

*This book is dedicated to the memory
of my friend Bob Goldham, and to
Vladimir Konstantinov. Both of these great
players were dedicated to the sport of
pro hockey, to their families, to the city
of Detroit, and to their teammates.*

Contents

4

A Triumphant Decade

5

Howe Leads the Way

Changes at the Top

Ilitch Takes Charge

The Cup Comes Home

Foreword

NOW in their seventy-third consecutive year in the National Hockey League, the Detroit Red Wings have compiled an illustrious record in what I genuinely feel is the world's greatest game. It is no exaggeration to call the Wings the leading producer of records, awards, and championships among all of the U.S. members of the NHL. The Red Wings have captured the coveted Stanley Cup on eight occasions.

I was fortunate to be part of a Detroit dynasty, when the Wings finished in first place seven consecutive times and skated off with four Cup victories. In 1952, we captured the Cup in eight consecutive playoff games. Terry Sawchuk, our goaltender, was magnificent that spring, compiling four shutouts and allowing only five goals. Those long-ago triumphs provide wonderful memories for me, for my teammates, and for the loyal fans on both sides of the border, fans who have always been there for us.

Many of the greatest Red Wing moments — and one or two I'd rather forget — are chronicled in these pages by my longtime friend Brian McFarlane, a Hall of Fame historian and my former broadcast partner on NBC. I know you are going to enjoy these tales of Adams, Sawchuk, Howe, Delvecchio, Goldham, Yzerman, and, yes, even Bob Probert and Howie Young. You may even find a yarn or two about a temperamental left winger who was often referred to as Terrible Ted or Scarface.

As the millennium approaches, the Red Wings once again appear to be on a high, winning the 1997 Stanley Cup in four straight games and coming right back in 1998. I wish them continued success, the kind our gang enjoyed in the late forties and fifties.

The Red Wings have always been close to my heart, always

intertwined with every aspect of my life. I was blessed to be able to begin and end my career in a Red Wing uniform. As a proud participant in one of the truly great franchises in the NHL, as a player, coach, general manager, and fan, I couldn't have wished for a better, longer, or more fulfilling career in the game I love than when I was a Red Wing.

Ted Lindsay
May 1998

Acknowledgments

MANY thanks to Steve Dryden, editor in chief of the *Hockey News*, and to the Hockey Hall of Fame and Museum. I would also like to thank Gordie and Colleen Howe, Red Storey, Marcel Pronovost, Johnny Wilson, Ted Lindsay, Marcel Bonin, Pete Stemkowski, Frank Mahovlich, and the late Bob Goldham, as well as Paul Patskou and Eric Bulmash for their assistance in compiling these Red Wing anecdotes.

1

The Early Years

Adams Wanted To Be a Surgeon

JOHN James Adams, one of six children born to John and Sarah Adams, wanted to become a surgeon when he grew up. Told that medical school was an expensive proposition, he laughed. He already knew how to make a quick buck, how to make ends meet. Hadn't he paid for his first pair of skates by selling newspapers, often in temperatures of thirty below zero, in Fort William, Ontario (now called Thunder Bay)? Hadn't he bribed the guard at the local arena to let him onto the ice to practice his hockey skills by slipping him cigar butts he'd scrounged from a local saloon?

Adams's medical hopes were sidetracked when the skills he mastered with stick and puck brought him, as a teenager, to Calumet, Michigan, one season. There he played hockey with a talented American, George Gipp, who went on to become a football hero at Notre Dame and the subject of the famous phrase, "Win one for the Gipper." Adams would tell his friends, "If you could skate and fight you could play there [Calumet] forever." Adams was no slouch at either.

Eventually he wandered east and joined teams in Peterborough and Sarnia. Just before the conclusion of the 1917–18 NHL season, he was recruited by the Toronto Arenas. In his first game, played in Montreal, he scored a hat trick and was almost slashed to ribbons for his audacity. Taken to hospital to have his facial wounds stitched up, the nurse on duty turned out to be his sister. His face was such a mess that she failed to recognize him.

World War I interrupted Jack's career. After his discharge from the Canadian army, he played briefly with Toronto, then jumped to Lester and Frank Patrick's Pacific Coast Hockey Association. One year he led Vancouver in penalty minutes, while the next season he led his team in goals with 25 in 24 games.

By 1922–23 he was back in Toronto, where he played for the St. Pats for four seasons. He finished his playing career at age 31 with the Ottawa Senators, whom he helped to win the 1927 Stanley Cup.

Shortly after those playoffs, Jack Adams learned that the Detroit hockey club, then known as the Cougars, had taken a financial bath after their first year in the NHL, losing $85,000.

"They need someone like me to run that club," a cocky Adams told NHL president Frank Calder. "I could do a good job there."

Calder agreed and told the Detroit owners they couldn't go wrong if they hired Adams.

At first Jack was surprised to hear his players booed in their home rink, the spanking new Olympia. Hundreds of fans would cross the river from Windsor, Ontario, hoping to see the home team get pummelled by the Canadian teams. It would be a long time before these fans would switch their allegiance to Detroit.

Adams soon found that managing a professional hockey team was not as easy as he had thought. Only once in his first four years on the job did his club finish higher than fourth in the American Division. And the team was constantly in financial trouble. More than once Adams had to put up some of his own money to meet the payroll.

Adams's Teams Were Awesome

MANAGER Jack Adams was one of the most successful executives in the history of the NHL. After joining Detroit as coach and general manager in 1927, his teams won seven Stanley Cups and 12 league titles.

From 1949 to 1955, his Detroit Red Wings finished in first place seven years in a row, a rate of success even baseball's New York Yankees couldn't claim.

He often boasted that "our 1951–52 team that won the play-offs in eight straight games was the greatest hockey team ever assembled."

Adams was the innovator of hockey's farm system, from which he harvested such stars as Gordie Howe, Terry Sawchuk, and Sid Abel.

His greatest satisfaction came from picking a raw-boned kid out of a Detroit training camp and watching him develop into the dominant player of his era. The youngster's name was Gordie Howe, who signed with Adams for a pittance — and the promise of a Red Wing hockey jacket worth $14.

For many years, the admiration between Howe and Adams was mutual. Gordie once said if he didn't have such wonderful parents back home in Saskatoon, he'd be proud to be known as a son to his manager, coach, and advisor.

Despite his nickname, "Jolly Jack" could be a ruthless adversary. He shunted Ted Lindsay, his great left winger, off to Chicago when Lindsay became president of a fledgling players' association. Adams detested unions and considered Lindsay's motives treasonous.

"Hockey's the greatest game there is," Adams once said. "It has to be to survive the number of jerks that are in it."

He fought with players and coaches on other teams and he

was known to invade the referees' room on occasion to deliver a stern lecture to a fuming arbiter. He once called Montreal's Rocket Richard a "hatchet man" after Richard collided with Marcel Pronovost and knocked out a couple of the Detroit defenseman's teeth. Richard replied, "Adams is full of baloney."

Adams was dropped as Detroit's general manager after the 1961–62 season, when he was 66 years old. His contributions to the game earned him the Lester Patrick Memorial Trophy in 1965, the first winner of the trophy awarded annually for long and meritorious service to hockey in the United States. He had been ushered into the Hockey Hall of Fame in 1959. Adams died of a heart attack on May 1, 1968.

"I felt sick when I heard the news," said Gordie Howe. "When I joined the Detroit organization at age 16, he looked after me like I was his own son."

"This is a great personal loss for me," added Sid Abel. "Everything I have ever done in hockey has been with Mr. Adams."

Adams Leaps into the Fray

WHILE Jack Adams was a huge success as a hockey coach and manager, he could never erase from his mind the memory of his greatest failure — the inability to guide his team to win the 1942 Stanley Cup. His team had swept Boston aside in the Stanley cup semi-finals and had followed that up with three straight wins over Toronto in the finals. With 15 minutes to play in game four, the Red Wings led by a goal. But in those waning moments Toronto tied the score, then went ahead by a goal. When the Leafs held on to win, Adams was wild with rage. He leaped onto the ice and bulled his way into an altercation between game officials and several players. Adams was accused of throwing punches at referee Mel Harwood, a charge Adams denied. "He went out there to protect the referee," stated Jim Norris, then a vice-president of the Red Wings, his tongue tucked firmly in cheek.

Some reporters and columnists wrote scathing denunciations of Adams's behavior and asked that he be banned from hockey forever. When he threatened libel suits against them, they hastily penned apologies.

Several years later, Adams would tell Trent Frayne in *Maclean's* magazine, "The fourth game in that '42 series was the bitterest of my career. We were leading with 15 minutes to play, but we lost by a goal after some of the most incredible refereeing I've ever seen. When the fourth game ended, three of my players, Grosso, Wares, and Abel, surrounded the referee, Mel Harwood, at the exit gate. I went across the ice after them to pull them away and was charged with belting the referee. Actually, I didn't get within ten feet of him in the scuffling, but the league president, Frank Calder, suspended me for the balance of the series and fined Wares and Grosso $100 each. To me, the series seemed to be controlled by the Toronto newspapers and Conn Smythe. Their influence on Calder provided my darkest moment in hockey."

Jolly Jack's Incredible Goal

BACK in 1921, Jack Adams was a star forward on the Vancouver Millionaires of the Pacific Coast Hockey Association.

In the final game of the 1920–21 season, Vancouver beat Victoria 11–8 and, during that highscoring affair, Jack Adams scored a goal. This was no rare feat for Adams — he scored plenty — but this was one he, accidentally, put into his own net, past Hughie Lehman, his surprised netminder.

Since the gaffe had no bearing on the game's outcome, Adams's mistake was quickly forgotten. What makes it remarkable, even more than 75 years later, is that Adams, for reasons no one can account for today, received credit for the goal in the individual scoring race. In fact, the bizarre tally vaulted him into fifth place in the scoring race.

Well, Hello Dolly

EVEN the most knowledgeable Red Wing fan will be hard-pressed to answer this trivia question: Name the goalie who holds the record for the best single season goals-against average in team history.

If you guessed Sawchuk or Hall, Crozier or Osgood, or even good old Harry "Apple Cheeks" Lumley, you're wrong.

The chap's name is in our title above: Clarence "Dolly" Dolson. And after 60 years, his record remains unchallenged. As a rookie netminder in 1928–29 — when the Wings were known as the Detroit Cougars — Dolson, who came from parts unknown, put up an average of 1.43 with 10 shutouts in 44 games.

But Dolly's gaudy stats in his spectacular debut didn't convince general manager Jack Adams that he would become another Georges Vezina. Two years later, the Ottawa Senators suspended operations and Adams grabbed their ace netminder, Alex Connell, in an early day dispersal draft.

Adams's choice was a good one. Thanks to Connell, the Red Wings crept back into the playoffs after a two-year absence.

Connell might have been a Detroit mainstay for many years to come. But Ottawa decided to rejoin the NHL for the 1932–33 season, and the Senators demanded the return of Connell. Adams acquired 12-year veteran John Ross Roach from the Rangers to replace him.

Somehow, somewhere, "Dolly" Dolson got lost in the shuffle. After being cut loose by Detroit he never played another NHL game.

Detroit's Other Howe

AS the 1971–72 season approached, there was something missing from the Red Wing roster: the name Howe was gone. For the previous 36 seasons a Howe had sparkled for Detroit — Gordie, of course, for 25 seasons from 1946–47 to 1970–71, and Syd Howe from 1934–35 to 1945–46. Both had been huge fan favorites, both had been team scoring leaders — Gordie 17 times, Syd three times — and both had been team captains — Syd in 1941–42 and Gordie from 1958–59 to 1961–62.

Not only was Syd Howe not related to Gordie Howe, he contrasted sharply to the greatest Red Wing scorer of them all. Syd was a comparatively small forward (five foot nine and 165 pounds) and a left-handed shot who seldom stood out in a crowd. Gordie had a mean streak while Syd was so well behaved on the ice that he was often a candidate for the Lady Byng Trophy. But Syd could score goals. And set them up.

Syd Howe broke into the NHL with Ottawa (his home town) in 1929–30 as an 18 year old. But the team's owners, in deep financial trouble, sold him to the Philadelphia Quakers, a team so devoid of talent they won a mere four games in 44 starts and then folded. Howe moved on to Toronto for three games, then was called back to Ottawa for a couple of seasons. When Ottawa dropped out of the NHL in 1934, most of the Senators were transferred to a new team in St. Louis, the Eagles. But the Eagles, like the Quakers, were as short on skill as they were on cash. Once again, young Howe found himself on a last-place club.

Still, his improved play caught the sharp eye of Detroit manager Jack Adams. When the Eagles served notice they were folding after the 1934–35 season, Adams forked over $50,000 in midseason for Howe and another player, Ralph "Scotty" Bowman (no relation to Detroit coach Scotty Bowman).

From the moment he donned the red and white jersey, Howe began to sparkle, at first on a line with Larry Aurie and Ebbie

Goodfellow and later with Mud Bruneteau and Wally Kilrea. By the end of the 1934–35 season, he had clicked for a total of 22 goals and 47 points and had finished second in the individual scoring race behind Charlie Conacher of the Leafs.

Howe's offensive spark helped propel the Wings to consecutive first-place finishes in their division over the next two seasons, as well as back-to-back Stanley Cups. They were the first Cup wins in Detroit history and, after the second one — a three-games-to-two squeaker over the Rangers, manager Adams became so excited that he passed out and had to be revived with smelling salts.

On January 29, 1942, Howe turned in a performance that surprised and delighted his fans. It was Syd Howe Night at the Olympia, and he was presented with a piano, among other gifts. He played the piano briefly at centre ice and waved to the crowd. Later, Howe scored both goals in a 2–0 Detroit victory.

Howe's biggest individual moment came years later, during the 1943–44 season. On February 3, 1944, he scored six times as Detroit plastered New York 12–2. It was not the most goals ever scored in a game — that mark belongs to Joe Malone, who scored seven for Quebec in a 1920 match. But it's been called a "modern day" record because he did it after 1927, when the modern era began. Howe's record later was matched by Red Berenson of the St. Louis Blues (against Philadelphia in 1968) and by Leaf captain Darryl Sittler (against the Boston Bruins in February 1976).

When he quit the game in 1946, Syd Howe reigned as hockey's all-time highest scorer with 528 points in 691 games. As Syd Howe walked away from the Olympia, another Howe was being greeted at the dressing-room door. This Howe would also one day reign as hockey's highest scorer.

2

Jim Norris at the Helm

Big Jim Norris Steps In

MONTREAL-born James E. Norris, czar of the multimillion-dollar Norris Grain empire, which included Great Lakes freighters, a railroad, and three huge cattle ranches, was a benevolent despot who loved hockey. He even had a small rink built on his estate in Lake Forest, Illinois, where his kids learned to play and enjoy the game. If someone was interviewed for a job as the Norris chauffeur or butler, one of the first questions asked was, "Can you skate?" because their duties included playing shinny with the Norris offspring.

For a couple of seasons Norris ran an outlaw team in Chicago that competed with the NHL Blackhawks for fan support. He put in a bid for a second NHL team in Chicago, but it was rebuffed. Furious, he blamed the Blackhawks owner, Major Frederick McLaughlin, for his exclusion.

In 1933, when he noticed the Detroit franchise was floundering financially, Norris stepped in and bought the club and its new home, the Olympia. He called Jack Adams into his office and barked, "You've got one year to make something of this. You're on probation. I'll give you the money, you build me a team."

Adams grinned and said, "Yes, sir." He knew he was talking to a man whose personality and hockey ambitions matched his own.

"Another thing we're gonna do," added Norris, "is change the name of this team. Forget about names of animals and birds like Cougars and Falcons. From now on it's going to be the Red Wings."

Norris, a defenseman with the Montreal Victorias in his youth, had grown up following another local team, the Winged

Wheelers. He liked the image of a wheel and felt it would be an ideal logo for Detroit, the automotive capital of the world.

Dipping into the immense Norris fortune, Adams began building a hockey dynasty. His team tied for the American Division title in 1932–33, won the division crown the following year, and captured the Stanley Cup in 1936, defeating Toronto three games to one.

His team suffered an extraordinary number of injuries in 1936–37 but still managed to finish atop the NHL standings. Adams had only a dozen healthy players going into the finals against the New York Rangers. Out with a broken leg was Larry Aurie, who'd led the league in goal scoring with 23, and Vezina Trophy–winning goaltender Normie Smith had a severe elbow injury. Despite the manpower shortage, Adams's team stubbornly made its way to a Cup victory in five games, becoming the first NHL club to win both the league title and the Stanley Cup in consecutive years. By then, Adams's "probation" had long since been served.

Meanwhile, Big Jim Norris had expanded his sports holdings. When real estate values crashed during the Great Depression, he purchased the $6-million Chicago Stadium for about a tenth of its original cost. It was sweet revenge for McLaughlin's earlier veto of a second Chicago club. He also became the largest stockholder in New York's Madison Square Garden, and he had interests in stadiums in St. Louis and Indianapolis. He was joined in the business by his son James D. Norris, who as head of the International Boxing Club, had a virtual stranglehold over prizefighting in the United States — backed, it has been alleged, by ties to the mob.

To "Big Jim" Norris, hockey was the king of sports. He insisted his players leave a good impression, and ordered them to wear a suit and tie and well-polished shoes on road trips.

He was told not to attend games of his beloved Red Wings for fear the excitement would put too much strain on his weak heart. The senior Norris died in hospital of a heart attack on December 4, 1952, and was succeeded as president of the Red Wings by his 25-year-old daughter, Marguerite. She was described by one of her employees as "a good looker, a regular person, and an avid hockey fan."

Frank Selke, Sr., once called James E. Norris "one of hockey's greatest individual figures. Away from NHL meetings he was all-Detroit. At meetings, he was all-league."

The Strange Career of Goalie Norman Smith

NORMIE Smith was having a good first season in the NHL, until he ran into Howie Morenz — or rather, Morenz ran into him. The rookie goaltender broke in with the Montreal Maroons in 1931 and played 20 games before, one night, Howie Morenz, the dazzling Canadiens' star, was sent flying into the Maroons' net. His fall was broken by Smith, who was injured so badly he was out for the rest of the season.

Smith spent the next two seasons in the minors, learning how to handle rebounds. He also discovered that wearing a peaked cap over his eyes cut down the glare from the overhead lights, allowing him to follow the play more easily. In 1934, Jack Adams signed him. Adams was soon displeased with Smith's play and he brought in John Ross Roach to take over for the second half of the 1934–35 season.

Smith got a second chance the following year and was in the Detroit goal for one of the most remarkable games ever played. After the Wings and the Maroons finished on top of their respective divisions (the Wings with 56 points, the Maroons with 54) they met in Montreal in the first round of the Stanley Cup play-offs. On March 24, 1936, Smith and Lorne Chabot were in their respective nets when the teams faced off at the Montreal Forum before more than 9,000 fans. Many of those fans would not be around for the finish of the match — they would be back home and fast asleep when the Wings' Mud Bruneteau scored the game's only goal at 2:25 a.m. — at 16:30 of the *sixth* overtime period. Norm Smith had recorded a shutout in the longest game ever played, 176 minutes and 30 seconds. Years later, editors from the *Guinness Book of World Records* also listed Smith's 92 saves in that game as a world record.

Smith's mastery over the Maroons continued into game two of the series, played two nights later at the Forum. He chalked up his second consecutive shutout when the Red Wings outscored the Maroons 3–0.

In game three, back in Detroit, the Maroons' Gus Marker finally put a puck past Smith in the first period, ending Smith's shutout streak at 248 minutes and 32 seconds. But Johnny Sorrell and Scotty Bowman (not to be confused with the current Red Wing coach of the same name) replied for the Wings, who won the game 2–1, ending the series.

The Red Wings went on to defeat Toronto in the finals, three games to one, and skated off with the Stanley Cup.

The next year, thanks largely to Smith, who won the Vezina Trophy, the Red Wings repeated as league champions. In the playoffs that spring, Smith suffered an elbow injury in game three against the Canadiens and was forced to the sidelines. He came back for game five and was in the net for a Detroit win that required 52 minutes of overtime.

In the finals against the Rangers, his sore elbow acted up, keeping him on the sidelines. Rookie netminder Earl Robertson took over and played a starring role as the Red Wings won their second straight Stanley Cup.

The Wings slipped badly in 1937–38, missing the playoffs and plummeting to the American Division basement.

Smith played just four games for Detroit in 1938–39, then one night he bolted from the team after a game in New York. Adams suspended him and quickly acquired veteran Tiny Thompson from Boston to replace him. Smith concluded that his NHL career was over.

But was it?

Five seasons went by and, desperate for goaltending help during World War II, Adams remembered Smith and invited him back. He played a mere five games in 1943–44 and one more the following season, and was then discarded. His NHL career wasn't long, only 198 games. But he did win a Vezina Trophy and two Stanley Cups, and he'll always be remembered as the winning goalie in the longest game ever played. No other netminder has come close to the playoff record he established over six decades ago — over nine periods of shutout hockey.

The Night Bucko
Bashed the Maroons

BUCKO McDonald was in his second year as an NHL defenseman when his Detroit Red Wings clashed with the Montreal Maroons in the opening round of the 1936 playoffs.

Bucko loved to hit, and before the first game at the Montreal Forum, a fan offered him five dollars for every Maroon he sent crashing to the ice. Neither the fan nor Mcdonald could have foreseen that the game would last longer than any in history — it would be nine periods before a winner could be declared.

From the opening whistle, Bucko enthusiastically sought out his targets and sent them sprawling, while in the stands the fan kept score. The game finally ended on Mud Bruneteau's goal at 16:30 of the sixth overtime period, giving Detroit a 1–0 victory. By that time, Bashing Bucko had been credited with 37 body-checks. The fan was happy to settle up with McDonald in the dressing room after the game, handing over the grand sum of $185.

The War Years and Beyond

Harry Lumley:
Another Goaltending Great

HARRY Lumley sits next to Johnny Bower at a long table in a Toronto hotel, signing autographs at a sports card show. As each fan approaches — and there are many, each one holding out a photo, a book, or a stick — Lumley greets them warmly. He's pleased they remember him, even though most are too young to ever have seen him play.

His signature is bold and beautiful. Having both his names end in a *y* gives him an opportunity to extend the tail of each letter, with a flourish, into two graceful lines that curve back toward the first letters in the names.

I ask him about his NHL debut with the Detroit Red Wings. It was in 1943–44, the middle of World War II, and, he recalls, "there was a real shortage of players. I was just a kid from Owen Sound — seventeen years old — and I'd just turned pro with Indianapolis. In no time at all Mr. Adams called me up to Detroit and I got a chance to play in a couple of games. I was very nervous and I didn't play very well at all. Lost both games and let in a lot of goals."

I'd been under the impression that his first NHL game had been for an opposing team later that season, the Rangers, coming down out of the stands to substitute for injured New York goalie Ken "Tubby" McAuley.

"No, no," he corrects me. "That didn't happen until later. That was my third game in the league."

The following season, 1944–45, Lumley played in 37 games with the Red Wings, and suddenly the rookie found himself playing for the Stanley Cup. After the Red Wings ousted Boston in seven games, they met the Maple Leafs in the finals.

Lumley's play in the first three games was impeccable, but Toronto's Frank McCool was unbeatable: the Wings lost by scores of 1–0, 2–0, and 1–0. Three games, three consecutive shutouts for McCool. The Red Wings finally found the net in game four, rolling to a 5–3 win to prolong the series. Then it was Lumley's turn to record a shutout — his first in playoff hockey — in a 2–0 win in game five. To prove it was no fluke he came right back in the sixth game with a 1–0 victory, and the series was tied at three games apiece.

The seventh game was played at the Detroit Olympia on April 22, 1945, and both goalies were spectacular. But it was McCool who prevailed in a 2–1 Toronto victory.

Players from both teams gathered at center ice as NHL president Frank Calder presented the Stanley Cup to the new champions. But the ceremony was overshadowed by an uproar from the stands. The crowd was chanting, "We want Lumley! We want Lumley!"

Harry Lumley had bolted for the Red Wing dressing room immediately after the final whistle. Crushed, and blaming himself for the loss, he sat alone, a picture of dejection. His teammates found him, lifted him to his feet, and escorted him back to the ice, where he received an ovation unlike any he'd ever heard.

Overcome with emotion, he waved to the fans and vowed that someday he'd reward them with a Stanley Cup. Five years later, in 1950, he kept his promise, leading Detroit to a seven-game triumph over the New York Rangers.

No sooner did that happen than, with rookie Terry Sawchuk waiting in the wings, Jack Adams sold Lumley to Chicago.

Stewart, Orlando in Bloody Battle

O N November 7, 1942, the Red Wings visited Maple Leaf Gardens in Toronto for a game against the defending Stanley Cup champions. One of the best Leafs was winger Gaye Stewart, winner of the Calder Trophy (over Rocket Richard, no less) as the NHL's top rookie the previous season.

On defense for Detroit was belligerent Jimmy Orlando, in his final season. Montreal-born Orlando was a hardrock who took great joy in leveling opposing forwards, especially newcomers like Stewart.

During this first meeting of the season between the arch-rivals, Stewart dashed down the boards only to be dumped heavily into the corner by Orlando's solid check. Stewart jumped to his feet and nailed Orlando with a two-handed slash with his stick. Orlando laughed as referee King Clancy blew his whistle and ordered Stewart to the penalty box.

Orlando describes what happened next:

"There he is in the penalty box, fuming like an enraged bull. Stewart was so mad he couldn't sit down. When play resumed I could hear him hollerin' at me so I hollered a few things back and he didn't like that one bit. Then — can you believe it? — he jumped out of the box and raced toward me. I'd never seen anything like it. The guy still had over a minute to serve in his penalty. Anyway, I see him coming so I drop my gloves and nail him a good one, sending him sprawling to the ice. Clancy don't see this because he's way up the ice with everybody else. Then Stewart jumps up, takes his stick, and smashes me right across the skull — a vicious blow that cut me for 23 stitches, I found out afterwards. I was in no man's land for the next few minutes so I never got to smack him back with my stick much, as I would have liked to. Clancy gave us both match penalties and the league fined us each $100. I was suspended from playing in Toronto the rest of the season and Stewart was banned from playing in Detroit, but somehow these suspensions were rescinded. By the way, somebody took a photo of me being led off the ice and it looks like I'd just been hit by a bus. Hockey was a tough game in those days."

Howe a Red Wing, Thanks to Selke

JACK Adams always took credit for finding, signing, and developing Gordie Howe into the greatest player of his era. But it's not generally known how close the big winger came to being a Toronto Maple Leaf. In his book *Red's Story*, former referee Red Storey tells how Frank Selke — executive assistant to Leaf owner Conn Smythe — went to Omaha on a scouting trip during the 1945–46 season. Selke was there to check on the progress of a couple of aspiring NHLers, the Morrison brothers, but the player who really caught his eye was 17-year-old Howe, then just beginning his professional career. On the way back to Toronto, Selke stopped off at the Detroit Olympia to meet with Jack Adams. They talked of the Morrison boys, then Selke mentioned Howe.

"Have you got that big guy on your protected list?" he asked.

Adams confessed that he didn't. Selke gave him some friendly advice.

"Get him on your list by midnight tonight. If you don't he'll be on the Toronto list by tomorrow and you'll be out of a job."

Adams took the advice but, Storey observes, "If their roles had been reversed, would Adams have issued a warning to Selke? No sir, he would have stolen Howe from under the noses of the Leafs."

Storey also perpetuates the oft-told tale that Jack Adams placed a contract in front of Howe each year and said "Gordie, fill in the blanks." Even when he was the game's brightest star, Gordie would never fill in an amount in excess of $1,000. "Never happened," says Howe today. "I'd get a small raise each year but as for blank contracts, Adams never put one of those in front of me."

One thing Storey can attest to was Gordie's unselfishness. He recalls the 1952–53 season, when Howe had 49 goals and 50 was a total only Rocket Richard had ever achieved. Late in the season, on a breakaway and with an empty net in front of him, Howe passed off to Alex Delvecchio, giving up a goal he could easily have scored himself. A game or two later, he tipped in a shot from the point by Red Kelly, but the referee missed the tip-in and awarded the goal to the redhead. Howe shrugged and didn't think to complain.

Remembering a Great

ELLIE Goldham called me on a Friday morning in September 1991 with devastating news. Her loving husband Bob was dead of a stroke at age 69. Tears fell freely at both ends of the line and she asked me to prepare a eulogy for the memorial service.

Every pew in the church was filled that day and I was amazed at how many former Red Wings had traveled to Toronto to pay their respects. It shouldn't have been a surprise; every teammate he'd ever played with had loved and respected the big defenseman.

There was never any danger of an inflated ego with Bob, I told those assembled. Only others thought him a rare and special individual.

Right from the beginning Bob wanted to be a hockey player. Perhaps his dream began one exciting day in the early thirties, when he rode in from Georgetown, Ontario, sitting on an apple crate in the back of a truck to see his first NHL game at Maple Leaf Gardens. No doubt he watched in amazement as the Kid Line and King Clancy performed their heroics on the ice below. If he happened to gaze up to the broadcast gondola that night, where Foster Hewitt sat hunched over a microphone describing the play in his inimitable fashion, it probably would never have occurred to young Goldham, even for a second, that many decades later he would occupy a seat there, where his wit and expert analysis would become an integral part of *Hockey Night in Canada*.

Bob must have known at an early age that his dreams were all but hopeless. Of the thousands of young men playing hockey, only 120 were selected to play in the NHL in a season, and only 36 of those were defensemen. Nevertheless, young Bob Goldham made up his mind to practice longer and harder than the other boys, to focus his energy on becoming one of the elite 30 or so.

And eventually he did.

His indoctrination into the National Hockey League came as a 19-year-old rookie, playing for the Toronto Maple Leafs. Seeing action in 19 games, he was slated, as most rookies are, to spend the 1942 Stanley Cup finals watching from the bench.

Goldham looked on in frustration as his teammates lost three straight games to the Red Wings. The Leafs were about to be swept into oblivion, when coach Hap Day made some desperate moves. He benched scoring ace Gordie Drillon and veteran defenseman Bucko McDonald, and called on Goldham and other bench-warmers to try to help avoid disaster.

In game four, Goldham excelled on defense and the Leafs came from behind for a 4–3 victory. The Leafs added rookie Gaye Stewart to the lineup for game five and cruised to a 9–3 win. Goldham contributed a goal and an assist. In game six, Goldham scored a key goal in a 3–0 win and the series was suddenly even. Detroit took a 1–0 lead into the third period of game seven, but Goldham set up another huge goal en route to a 3–1 win as the Leafs engineered the greatest playoff comeback in NHL history. Could any rookie have asked for a more exciting debut?

Goldham barely had time to savor the moment when he was asked to switch uniforms, and he went from Maple Leaf blue to navy blue. After three years of wartime service, Bob returned to the

Leafs. Later that year, he was involved in one of hockey's biggest trades when he was shipped, along with Gus Bodnar, Ernie Dickens, Gaye Stewart, and Bud Poile, to Chicago in return for the Hawks's dipsy-doodling centerman, Max Bentley, and journeyman forward Cy Thomas.

A subsequent trade brought Goldham to Detroit, where he performed with some of the greatest stars in the game — Sawchuk, Howe, Abel, Lindsay, and Kelly — all future Hall of Famers. By then Goldham had become a master of the blue line and a key performer in Detroit's Stanley Cup win in 1952, achieved in the minimum of eight games. He spent half of his 12-year career in a Detroit uniform and became one of the most popular Red Wings of all time. Chroniclers of the game often wonder why Goldham, with his uncanny ability to drop down and block shots, with his remarkably solid play, has not been inducted into the Hockey Hall of Fame. The modest Goldham would never have suggested nor sought such recognition for himself. He was proud to be known as a team player, satisfied to turn in an honest performance night after night.

In one of Goldham's post-NHL endeavors, he joined the staff of *Hockey Night in Canada*. The producers had hired Bob to replace me as color commentator on Maple Leaf telecasts, but he refused to accept the assignment until he talked with me.

"Brian," he said, "I'd never seek or take a job from another person if it would hurt them. If it turns out it's between you and me for the job, I'll simply tell them I'm not interested in the position."

As it turned out, things worked out and there was room for both of us on the telecasts.

Flashback to a Rout

ON January 23, 1944, the Red Wings met the New York Rangers at the Olympia. Nobody could have anticipated the impending offensive outburst by Detroit. After two periods, the Wings held a 7–0 lead. If that wasn't enough, in the third they set an NHL record for goals in a period with eight, en route to a 15–0 humiliation of the Rangers and their crestfallen netminder, Ken McAuley. An oddity fixed to that game is that Ranger coach Frank Boucher couldn't be blamed for the defeat. He had been called home to Ottawa for his brother's funeral and missed the most lop-sided game in history. Manager Lester Patrick had volunteered to hold the coaching reins in his place. "It'll be fun to coach again," Patrick told Boucher. Ten different Red Wings scored in the contest, led by a Syd Howe hat trick. Connie Dion recorded the shutout, the only one of his 38-game NHL career.

Detroit's 15 goals are not the most ever scored by one team in an NHL game. That honor goes to the Montreal Canadiens, who, on March 3, 1920, blasted the Quebec Bulldogs 16–3. The Wings did, however, set a record — still standing — for the most *consecutive* goals in one game. Over the years, four other teams would equal Detroit's mark of eight goals in a period, before the Buffalo Sabres broke the record on March 19, 1981, scoring nine times in a 14–4 rout of the Maple Leafs.

Wings First with Firewagon Hockey

DURING the 1940–41 NHL season, Detroit coach Jack Adams found himself with a team of aggressive players who checked with a vengeance. They may not have been as skilled or speedy as their NHL rivals, but their rambunctious play soon changed the face of the game. Montreal coach Dick Irvin would later adapt the Red Wings' style to his Canadiens and give it a name: firewagon hockey.

Adams had a lean centerman named Don "The Count" Grosso, who was a determined forechecker. Adams decided to build his team's offensive strategy around Grosso. Ever since the forward pass was legalized, teams carried or passed the puck into the offensive zone. The Red Wings began to shoot the puck in, and all five skaters would pour into the attacking zone. Other teams had used this approach on the power play, but the Wings began to do it all the time.

With Grosso leading the way, the Wings created trouble for everyone. Speedy centers like Toronto's Syl Apps or Boston's Milt Schmidt would circle behind their net, preparing for a rink-length rush — and find Grosso and Company blocking their way.

At first the experts jeered the Wings. Toronto fans and players called it "hooligan's hockey." The critics were less vocal two years later when the Red Wings' new style brought them a Stanley Cup in a four-game sweep of the Boston Bruins.

This aggressive forechecking resulted in one of the most important rule changes of the century — the introduction of the center red line. "Too much of the game is being played in the defensive zones," Ranger coach Frank Boucher explained. "If teams can pass all the way up to the new red line, it'll take the pressure off. It'll help them cope with the strong forechecking of the Red Wings."

Owner's Son Jumps Ref

THE Red Wings were involved in a riotous game at the Chicago Stadium on February 16, 1947, which they would lose, when Blackhawk defenseman Bill Gadsby's goal snapped a 2–2 tie with only two seconds left on the clock.

The winning goal came after a free-for-all that saw referee King Clancy hand out six major penalties and a pair of misconducts. Naturally, Ted Lindsay was one of the main combatants and so was Chicago's hulking Johnny Mariucci. What made this rumpus unique was a sudden and unprovoked attack on Clancy — not by one of the players, but by a young man who hustled out on the ice from the stands. This assault brought a roar from Detroit manager Jack Adams, who hopped over the boards and skidded along the ice toward Clancy. "I didn't go out there to hit him, I went out to save him," Adams explained later. "I couldn't bear to see that young jackass attack my old pal Clancy."

And who was the young jackass? He turned out to be the son of Irene Castle, the famous dancer — and her husband, Blackhawks owner Frederick McLaughlin. When the rhubarb was over, Clancy assessed $25 fines against all the players who left their benches. But he was at a loss for what do about the boss's son. "A good swift kick in the ass is what he deserved," the King would mutter afterward.

Adams a Lousy Hockey Man, Lindsay Says

OVER the years Red Wing GM Jack Adams won many accolades for his intelligent handling of the Detroit hockey club. A brilliant coach, manager, and executive, right? Wrong, according to Ted Lindsay and several other Red Wings.

"I say Adams was a lousy hockey man," states Lindsay angrily. "That's my opinion."

Linday is still incensed over the trade that sent him from Detroit to lowly Chicago, a deal precipitated by Lindsay's attempts to form a players' association. The most unforgivable aspect of that deal, Lindsay says, is that "Adams cheated me out of at least five and maybe as many as seven or eight Stanley Cups.

"After we won two Cups in a row in 1954 and 1955, he traded nine players away from the Red Wings. We could have stayed on top. Instead, we went downhill from there.

"What really rankles is the trade he didn't make. After we won in '55, the Canadiens wanted Terry Sawchuk. We could have parted with Terry because we had a great goaltender in the wings in Glenn Hall. And we could have had defenseman Doug Harvey in return. Adams refused to make the deal and the Habs went on to win five consecutive Stanley Cups with Harvey leading them every step of the way. He was the Bobby Orr of his era.

"Adams told somebody he wouldn't make the trade because he didn't want to make Montreal stronger. They won the next five Cups. How much stronger could they have become?"

Howe's Life-Threatening Injury

ORDIE Howe blossomed into a true superstar during the 1949–50 NHL season. He led the Red Wings in goals, with 35, and he finished third in the league in total points behind teammates Ted Lindsay and Sid Abel. His Red Wings led the league standings with 88 points — the most in NHL history to that date — and were favored to oust Toronto in the first round of the playoffs.

The opening game was played at the Olympia on March 28, 1950, and it was a double disaster for the Red Wings, who lost the match 5–0 and almost lost their brilliant right winger forever.

Fists flew early in that game as Howe battled Leaf tough guy Bill Juzda. Meanwhile, the Production Line of Howe, Ted Lindsay, and Sid Abel, who'd scored 92 goals between them in regular-season play, were stymied by the tight-checking Leafs and the goaltending of Turk Broda. The Wings had suffered through 11 straight playoff losses to Toronto and midway through the third period, it became clear the string would be extended to 12.

With minutes to go, Leaf captain Ted Kennedy, stickhandling along the boards through the neutral zone, was taken out of the play by both Howe and rugged defenseman Jack Stewart.

"I was going to run Kennedy into the boards," Howe recalls. "I was leaning forward, my head low to the ice, when Kennedy passed the puck to Sid Smith. Kennedy came around with the stick and spiked me right in the eye. The blow didn't lacerate the eye but it did some damage. The real damage came a second later when I crashed into the boards."

The crowd gasped as Howe nosedived into the boards and collapsed to the ice, unconscious. Moments later, he tried to get to his feet, then slumped back to the ice.

Team doctors and trainers diagnosed a broken nose, a possible broken cheekbone, damage to one eye, and a serious concussion. Howe was immediately taken by ambulance to Harper Hospital.

"I'll never forget that horrible ride," Howe would say. "People around me were saying, 'You're okay, Gord,' but I didn't feel okay. I felt terribly sick. At the hospital someone gave me a drink of water and I vomited. They rushed me into the operating room and I remember getting upset when they shaved my head. Even though the anesthetist was there I recall the shock of having a drill put to my skull and feeling the pressure and hoping they knew what they were doing and when to stop the drill."

Dr. Frederic Schreiber, a brilliant neurosurgeon, drilled a small opening in Gordie's skull above his right ear to relieve the pressure on his brain. Dr. Schreiber would later tell Ted Lindsay that if it had taken just 30 minutes longer to tend to Howe, he could easily have lost his life.

The Red Wings arranged for Gordie's mother and sister Gladys to fly from Saskatoon to Detroit. Mrs. Howe had been airsick all the way — it was her first flight — and she found her son weak but conscious, and with his sense of humor still intact.

"I told her she looked so ill from the trip that I'd better get up and let her take the bed," Gordie quipped.

Dr. Schreiber predicted a full recovery for his star patient and said Gordie could expect to play hockey again the following season.

Back at the Olympia the incident was not being forgotten quickly and some nasty accusations were aired. Red Wing coach Tommy Ivan denounced referee George Gravel for not calling a penalty on the play. Ivan claimed Kennedy had deliberately butt-ended his star forward. In his defense, Gravel said he hadn't seen any infraction of the rules. League president Clarence Campbell backed up his referee after watching game films.

Kennedy went as far as to offer to swear an oath that he had not intended to harm Howe. "I didn't even know he was hurt until I turned to come back down the ice and he was lying there, blood all over his face," the Leaf captain said.

"We had to get our act together for game two," Lindsay said. "It was a game we had to win and even though I hated Kennedy personally, I respected him as a player. He was a great one. We couldn't worry too much about getting even. Not then."

Late in the second period of game two, Lindsay was mugged by the Leafs' Gus Mortson. No penalty was called. Then Lee Fogolin of the Wings was sent off for tripping Kennedy. A furious Lindsay hauled Kennedy's skates out from under him and a dandy free-for-all broke out. Mortson whacked Lindsay, Fogolin attacked Mortson, and Bill Barilko traded punches with Marty Pavelich.

Regaining his feet, Kennedy found big Leo Reise in his sights and speared him. Reise used his stick to drop Jim Thomson with a head blow, then he ran the stick across Kennedy's neck. By then, Lindsay was on the loose and he charged into Kennedy, nailing him hard. Meanwhile, Mortson and Sid Abel squared off and belted each other.

Tempers flared later in the game. With Detroit leading 3–1, Bill Ezinicki assaulted Lindsay, cross-checking him to the ice. Lindsay jumped up, dropped his gloves, and charged Ezinicki. They fell to the ice, with Lindsay on top. Meanwhile, Vic Lynn decided he'd test mild-mannered Red Kelly and received quite a drubbing. When Bill Juzda saw a chance, he belted Lindsay and sent him to the ice.

When the dust cleared, the Red Wings had evened the series. They went on to eliminate the Leafs, propelled by Reise's overtime goal in the seventh game. When the Red Wings called Harper Hospital after the victory, Gordie surprised them by saying he'd watched the game on television.

Detroit took the final series over the Rangers, who hung on into double overtime in game seven before Red Wing Pete Babando scored the winner at 8:31 and the celebration began.

The crowd at the Olympia immediately began chanting "We want Howe!" and, moments later, Gordie emerged from the players' entrance, his head swathed in bandages. He received a tumultuous welome. With tears in his eyes he reached out to touch the Stanley Cup. It would not be the last time he placed a hand on it.

Jack Adams once scored a goal against his own goaltender — and it counted in the scoring race. He joined Detroit as manager–coach in 1927 and spent 35 years with the organization.   — Hockey Hall of Fame

e Goodfellow spent his entire career
 Detroit and played on three Stanley
-winning teams. He won the Hart
hy in 1940.   — Hockey Hall of Fame

oit's Jimmy Orlando is helped
he ice by referee King Clancy
r being bloodied by Toronto's
e Stewart in a slugfest during
1942–43 season.
ockey Hall of Fame

Modere "Mud" Bruneteau ended the longest game ever played when he scored against Maroons' goalie Lorne Chabot at 2:25 a.m. in the opening game of the 1936 semifinals. His shot ended 176 minutes and 30 seconds of play.   — Hockey Hall of Fame

Red Wing manager Jack Adams hugs goalie
Harry Lumley and forward Jud McAtee after
a winning effort during the 1945 playoffs.
Note the "V" for Victory logo on the jersey
sleeve, a patriotic symbol of wartime hockey.
— Hockey Hall of Fame

After long-time Detroit trainer Ross
"Lefty" Wilson was pressed into
service as a substitute goalie for the
Leafs one night, a humorous sports
editor had Wilson's photo doctored
fit the occasion. — Hockey Hall of Fa

In this game in the late 1950s, Earl "Dutch" Reibel is thwarted by Leaf goalie
Harry Lumley, a former Red Wing. — Hockey Hall of Fame

Legendary left winger Ted Lindsay dashes after a loose puck in front of Leaf netminder Ed Chadwick in a game in 1956. — Hockey Hall of Fame

John "Black Jack" Stewart was an
outstanding defenseman with the Red
Wings for ten seasons. He was inducted
into the Hockey Hall of Fame in 1964.
— Hockey Hall of Fame

Ted Lindsay emerged from a four-year
retirement as a player in 1964–65 and
helped the Red Wings to a league title.
He was inducted into the Hockey Hall of
Fame in 1966. — Hockey Hall of Fame

Referee Red Storey "explains" his call to Leaf goalie Harry Lumley and the
Wings' Ted Lindsay. — Hockey Hall of Fame

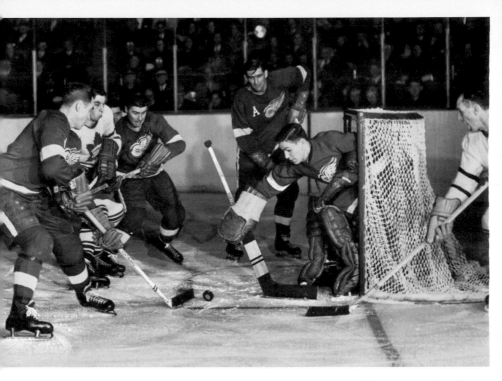

All-Star defenseman Red Kelly clears the puck from the Red Wing crease as goaltender Terry Sawchuk looks on. The Leafs' Ted Kennedy (far right) looks for a rebound.

— Hockey Hall of Fame

Gordie Howe was the most durable player in NHL history. He played 26 seasons in the NHL and 6 more in the WHA. Howe scored 786 of his 801 career goals as a Red Wing.

— Hockey Hall of Fame

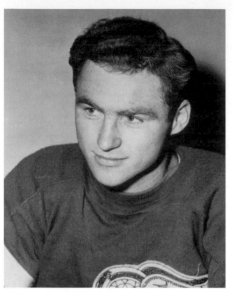

Defenseman Red Kelly was the first recipient of the James Norris Memorial Trophy as the NHL's top defenseman. He was the only non–Montreal Canadien to play on eight Stanley Cup–winning teams, four in Detroit and four more in Toronto.
— Hockey Hall of Fame

Defenseman Marcel Pronovost played on four Stanley Cup–winning teams in Detroit. In 1965 he was traded to Toron where he was a key member of the last Toronto team to win the Cup in 1967.
— Hockey Hall of Fame

Detroit's renowned Production Line: right winger Gordie Howe, center Sid Abel, and left winger Ted Lindsay. In 1949–50, the trio finished 1, 2, and 3 in the scoring race.
— Hockey Hall of Fame

Rookie Detroit coach Jimmy Skinner earns an embrace from manager Jack Adams after the Red Wings capture the 1955 Stanley Cup, defeating Montreal in seven games. — Hockey Hall of Fame

...seman Marcel Pronovost (#3) steps ...nt of Montreal's Jean Beliveau as ... Glenn Hall looks for the puck. Hall ...d with the Red Wings from 1952–53 ...gh 1956–1957. All three players ...on to the Hockey Hall of Fame. ...key Hall of Fame

Bruce Norris and his sister Marguerite (right) place their hands on the Stanley Cup as their sister-in-law looks on. Marguerite Norris was Red Wing president from 1952 to 1955 and was the first woman to have her name engraved on the famous trophy. — Hockey Hall of Fame

Defenseman Bill Quackenbush was a three-time All-Star and was an anchor on the Red Wing blueline in the 1940s and 1950s. — Hockey Hall of Fame

Goalie Terry Sawchuk fends off Floyd Curry and Paul Masnick of the Habs. In 1952, Sawchuk won eight straight playoff games, allowed only five goals, and collected four shutouts. — Hockey Hall of Fame

Terry Sawchuk ignores the Bruins' Leo Labine as Marcel Pronovost looks on. Pronovost and Bob Goldham (#2) helped make life easier for Sawchuk, who compiled a record 103 shutouts in his long career. — Hockey Hall of Fame

Was Howe Tough? I'll Say

WHEN Gordie Howe was a youngster his father gave him some good advice: never take any guff from anybody. One day Gordie witnessed firsthand what his dad meant. In a Saskatoon pool room one day, a guy annoyed the elder Howe by tapping his hand with a cue whenever he was lining up a shot. Gordie's dad straightened up and socked the joker, knocking him cold with the butt of his big hand.

Perhaps Gordie had his old man in mind whenever he ran into troublemakers on the ice. Instead of dropping his gloves and fighting, Gordie would let them know he was peeved by giving them a taste of his stick. Son Marty says his dad could cut an opponent for three stitches or five, depending on how annoyed he was.

One night during a game in the old World Hockey Association in Houston, Marty Howe found himself underneath a bigger, stronger opponent. One of Marty's teammates skated over and told the player holding Marty down to let him up. The opponent laughed and refused to let go.

Then big Gordie skated over and delivered the same message. Gordie was treated to a stream of obscenities. Gordie took off one glove, reached down, and pushed two fingers up the tough guy's nostrils. While the player screamed in pain, Gordie lifted him off Marty. Marty recalls the player bouncing to his feet, shouting, "I'm up! I'm up!" Only then did Gordie release the player to go to the penalty box, nursing a head that felt like a bowling ball.

Here's a list of injuries that slowed Gordie down — but not for long: A broken wrist; broken fingers; broken ribs; broken collarbone (undiagnosed for a year); broken toe (hit by a Bobby Hull slapshot); carpal tunnel surgery; nose broken 14 times; broken cheekbone, scratched eyeball, and severe concussion (all in the 1950 Ted Kennedy incident); broken foot; hernia; torn knee cartilage; and about 500 stitches to the face.

Ranger tough guy Leapin' Lou Fontinato took a run at Gordie one night at Madison Square Garden in February 1959. Fontinato sought revenge for a hard hit Howe had laid on Ranger rookie Eddie Shack. But Gordie saw the New York enforcer racing toward him. He stepped away from a Fontinato haymaker and came back with a flurry of punches thrown so hard that one of his fingers popped out of joint. Fontinato's nose was crushed and his face bloodied. To his credit, Fontinato finished the game.

Nearly 40 years later, people still talk about a photo printed the next day showing the damage to Fontinato's face. At the time, one of the game officials, Art Skov, said, "I grabbed Fontinato and he had his head down. Then he looked up. There was blood everywhere and it looked like his nose was gone. Then, when Fontinato was leaving the ice, Ranger coach Phil Watson grabbed him by the arm and lifted it up. Like he'd won the fight!"

Did Gordie feel any remorse? "No, none at all," he states. "Louie had been after me for years. He had it coming."

A Triumphant Decade

The Octopus Tossers

WHAT kind of people would stuff a slippery sea creature with eight sucker-bearing arms into a paper bag and take it to a hockey game? Detroit Red Wing fans would. They've been doing it for years, for almost half a century. Tossing a dead octopus onto the ice during Red Wings playoff games has become a bizarre tradition that can be blamed on (or credited to) the brothers Cusimano.

In 1952, Pete and Jerry Cusimano took a dead octopus (their father was in the fish business) to what turned out to be the final game of the Stanley Cup playoffs between the Red Wings and the Canadiens. The brothers reasoned that the eight tentacles of the octopus represented eight playoff victories, and since the Wings had already won seven straight playoff games, four over Toronto and three more over Montreal, the splat of an octopus hitting the ice might inspire them, or bring them luck, or shock or jinx the Habs. It might even lead to a final victory, to the Stanley Cup. Well, it seemed like a good idea at the time, if only to the Cusimanos.

But it worked. The Red Wings won the Cup with a 3–0 victory that night (although a more fitting score might have been 8–0). The octopus was given a bit of credit for the victory and the Cusimanos enjoyed some backslapping from their friends at the fish factory the next day.

"Too bad," said former NHL referee Red Storey, when the octopus tossing became a ritual every spring. "Those guys started a tradition that always made us officials a little uneasy during Detroit games. That damn thing would come flying out of the stands sometime during the first five minutes of play. I'd have one eye on the game and the other eye on the stands, wondering when those little buggers were going to throw that ugly thing. As a result, I seldom called any penalties early in the game. I was on octopus watch.

"Pick the damn thing up? Not me. I never went near them. Somehow, Marcel Pronovost got to be the picker-upper. It didn't bother him at all to scoop one of those weird looking things off the ice and toss it in the nearest garbage bin."

Budd Was the Best

DETROIT announcer Budd Lynch is as synonymous with the Red Wings as Foster Hewitt (his boyhood idol) was with the Leafs, or Danny Gallivan with the Canadiens. An eyewitness to one of the greatest dynasties in NHL history, Lynch called the play as the Red Wings swept to seven consecutive first-place finishes between 1949 and 1955. Four times during that stretch they skated off with the Stanley Cup.

Budd's arrival in the broadcast booth coincided with the introduction of television. During the 1949–50 season, TV station WWJ televised the last period and a half of 12 Detroit games and Lynch, recommended by Jack Adams, was hired to call the play. He made such a fine impression that radio station WXYZ signed him to announce all 70 games in 1950–51. He continued to cover the games on TV as well.

For 26 seasons Budd was the voice of the Red Wings. And when he left the booth after the 1974–75 season, Red Wings GM Alex Delvecchio asked him to stay on with the organization as public relations director — a job he held until 1982, when he took on a new role as the Wings' director of community relations.

Asked to name his best memory of Detroit hockey, Budd says, "I can never forget Tony Leswick's winning goal in overtime in the Stanley Cup finals of 1954. The Wings followed up with another Cup win in 1955, then Montreal took over and won a remarkable five in a row. We didn't win another Cup until 1997."

As for memorable people, Budd says, "I was privileged to see Gordie Howe play for most of his career. And it was always a thrill to watch the Production Line — Gordie, Ted Lindsay, and Sid Abel — when they dominated the league.

"I've always maintained that Jack Adams was the greatest personality of them all in my era, the best coach and general manager, the dominant force during those years of glory. He was the man who gave me my start in broadcasting. I'll be forever grateful to him for that."

And Detroit fans will always be grateful to Budd, an extraordinary broadcaster and a fixture on the city's sports scene for half a century.

The Joke's on Goldham

ORDIE Howe chuckles as he tells me about a practical joke he and his mates played on Red Wing star defenseman Bob Goldham one season.

"Bob's wife Ellie was in on it," recalls Howe. "She gave us the word that Bob would be wearing one of his favorite old suits on a road trip. He called it his lucky suit, believing that when he wore it the Wings would win. But it really was an ugly suit. Ellie gave us his measurements so we all chipped in and bought Bob another suit — an expensive one. We didn't tell him about it, though — not until we'd had some fun.

"When we were on the ice playing our next road game, Lefty Wilson, our trainer, snuck back to the dressing room and used a razor blade to cut the seams holding Bob's old suit together. After the game, Bob showered and slipped into his clothes. He put a leg into his pants and let out a howl when the seam came apart and the entire pant leg dropped to the floor. Then the other pant leg fell apart and he was left holding a bunch of cloth held up by his belt.

"Now he was mad because he knew we'd been up to something. He grabbed for his suit coat and one sleeve came away in his hand. The other sleeve started to come loose and the coat split up the back. Oh my, was he mad. Lefty Wilson came over and offered him some hockey tape. 'Maybe this will hold the suit together,' he said sympathetically. 'That was a dirty trick someone played on you.'

"Goldham was fuming, wondering how he'd ever be able to patch his ugly suit together, while the rest of us were falling over laughing. When his howls of outrage started to rattle the windows we marched over and presented Bob with the brand-new suit we'd bought him. We thought the gift would please him, and when he finally put it on it was a perfect fit. But he was still fuming over our little joke and didn't even thank us. 'I'll thank you so-and-so's when I cool off,' was all he muttered as he threw the old suit into a trash can."

Second Banana
a First-Class Guy

H E played in over 1,500 NHL games, scored 456 goals, and added 825 assists — all with the same team. Yet he's the number-two performer in each category on his team's all-time list. By now, any Detroit fan of a certain age knows we're referring to Alex Delvecchio, who spent his entire career on the ice under the monstrous shadow cast by Gordie Howe.

"It never really bothered me," Delvecchio says. "Gordie was

the greatest player of all time. When you played with him, and you gave him the puck, you just knew that some good things were going to happen for the Red Wings.

"As a centerman, I felt it was my job to make plays, to set up other players for the goals." Delvecchio placed a lot of emphasis on team play and sportsmanship. During his long career, he was a three-time winner of the Lady Byng trophy, awarded for "sportsmanship and gentlemanly conduct combined with a high standard of playing ability."

He played in the NHL for 24 seasons (two less than Howe) and is second only to Gordie in NHL history in games played — 1,767 to 1,549. What's truly remarkable is that, unlike most other NHLers noted for longevity — Howe, John Bucyk, Tim Horton — is that Delvecchio played his entire career with one team.

At one point in his career, Delvecchio contemplated changing teams. A year after Gordie Howe came out of retirement to play for Houston of the WHA, Alex Delvecchio was offered an enticing contract to jump to the Aeros. But after 24 seasons in Detroit, he decided he was "too old" to make the switch.

Delvecchio's career scoring stats might have been even more impressive if he hadn't encountered a bizarre slump during the 1969–70 season. He skated through the first 32 games of the season without scoring a goal. His goal famine became international news, and fans sent him dozens of good luck charms to help him snap the horrendous jinx. Then Miss America came to his aid: Pamela Anne Eldred, of Birmingham, Michigan, had worn a small jeweled pin on her brassiere when she captured the Miss America title. She sent the pin to Delvecchio and wished him luck. Alex attached the pin to his suspenders, and eureka! On New Year's Eve, 1969, he scored his first two goals of the season in a 5–1 rout of Boston. Three nights later, with the pin firmly in place, he scored a hat trick against Philadelphia. He connected 21 times in 41 games the rest of the way — his most prodigious rate ever.

Later, as a coach and general manager of the Red Wings in the mid '70s, Alex's easy-going style won the respect of the Detroit players. His hard-nosed predecessor, Ted Garvin, had insisted on a multitude of silly rules: no long hair, strict curfews with $500 fines to those who missed them, no players' children in the dressing room or on the ice. Delvecchio threw out the rules and quickly turned the team around, silencing the critics who said he was too nice to be a coach.

"He communicates," said winger Nick Libett. "Alex has class. He knows how to handle men. How could you not want to play for him?

On his office wall he hung a framed poem, one he could quote from memory, one that sums up his philosophy:

Sometimes when you're feeling important
Sometimes when your ego's in bloom,
Sometimes when you take it for granted
You're the best qualified in the room
Take a bucket and fill it with water
Put your hand in it up to the wrist
Pull it out and the hole that's remaining
Is a measure of how much you'll be missed

Billy Dea's Big Moment

LEFT winger Billy Dea's first season with Detroit in 1956–57 was a good one. He scored 15 goals in 69 games, an impressive total in those six-team days. The 15th and final goal of that season is one that Dea will always remember.

"I had a bonus for 15 goals that year, and coming into the last game of the season against Toronto I was stalled at 14. The Wings had first place locked up and Gordie Howe had the scoring title in the bag so (coach) Jimmy Skinner gave me a break. He said, 'Billy, you'll be playing with Gordie and Norm Ullman tonight.'

"Gordie's pre-game instructions were simple enough. 'Billy, stand in front of the net,' was about all he said. So I stood right where he told me to, nose to nose with the Toronto goalie, for two periods while Gordie and Normie fed me the puck. I must have had 15 shots on goal, and didn't score on any of them. Finally in the third period I put one in and I got my bonus. My arms were tired from all that shooting. I'll never forget how much effort Gordie put into feeding me those passes. Just so I could earn a little extra money. But that's the kind of guy big Gordie was."

Dea was traded to Chicago midway through the next season, played a few games, then drifted off to the American Hockey League for the next few years. In 1967–68, at age 34 and after a ten-year absence from the NHL, he re-surfaced with the expansion Pittsburgh Penguins and scored a career high 16 goals. At age 36, he rejoined Detroit and played two more seasons, ending his career after the 1970–71 season. He's one of the few NHL players to perform in more games in his 30's (251) than he did in his 20's (147).

On December 31, 1975, Dea joined the Red Wings coaching staff, assisting head coach Alex Delvecchio. He was let go on January 18, 1977. Five years later, on March 10, 1982, he was brought back as head coach, replacing Wayne Maxner. His team lost eight of eleven games, and Dea was dismissed for the second time in August 1982.

Delvecchio's Memorable Rookie Season

ALEX Delvecchio joined the Red Wings in 1951–52, fresh from the Oshawa Generals of the Ontario junior league. Never before, at any level of play, had the smooth center been part of a championship team, yet he was about to cap the first of his

23 NHL seasons as a member of one of the most remarkable Stanley Cup–winning teams ever.

The Red Wings, who ended the regular season on top of the NHL standings, faced Toronto in the semifinals. Opening at home, Delvecchio watched in amazement as Red Wing goalie Terry Sawchuk played a spectacular game and shut out the Leafs 3–0. In game two, Sawchuk put on another dazzling show, this time a 1–0 blanking of the blue and white.

The Leafs finally beat Sawchuk for a pair of goals in game three in Toronto, but the Red Wings humiliated Leaf goalie Turk Broda that night, winning easily 6–2. The Wings closed Toronto's season with a 3–1 victory in game four, then turned their attention to the powerful Montreal Canadiens.

The series opened at the Montreal Forum and Detroit got off to a fast start with a 3–1 victory. Ted Lindsay scored the winner in game two, a 2–1 squeaker. Back at the Olympia, Howe and Lindsay did all the goal scoring as Sawchuk came up with another shutout — 3–0 this time. Two nights later, Sawchuk blanked Montreal by the same score and the Wings had swept to the Stanley Cup in eight straight games. No team had ever won the Cup so easily, and none has so completely dominated the playoffs since.

Delvecchio had to pinch himself. "It really was a dream come true," he said. "It was the first time I'd been on a winning team of any kind and my first turned out to be a Stanley Cup winner. What a great feeling.

"Our fans in Detroit saw four home games but didn't see a single goal scored by our opponents," Delvecchio says. "Now that's some goaltending."

Little Tony Lights It Up

I
T had been the least productive of his nine NHL seasons —
just 6 goals in 70 games. So, as the 1954 playoffs began, little
Tony Leswick — all five foot six and 160 pounds of him —
understandably set out to redeem himself.

And he did. He scored goals in games one and three as the
Red Wings ousted Toronto in the opening round. But his biggest
marker was yet to come.

The final series against the Montreal Canadiens was a thriller.
It seesawed back and forth until the teams met in the seventh
and deciding game. A record crowd of 15,791 turned out at the
Detroit Olympia, and they were rewarded with a brilliant contest of speed and skill.

The Canadiens jumped to an early 1–0 lead on Floyd Curry's
goal. Red Kelly tied it for the Wings in the second. The teams
fought through the third period and on into overtime with both
clubs checking fiercely.

Montreal goalie Gerry McNeil, sidelined since February 11,
had replaced Jacques Plante for games five, six, and seven, and had
proved to be every inch the equal of Detroit's Terry Sawchuk.
Then, shortly after the four-minute mark of overtime, the Red
Wings got a break. Lanky center Glen Skov dashed to the end
boards behind McNeil, then turned and whipped a pass out to
Leswick, who was waiting in the faceoff circle about 30 feet
to McNeil's left. Leswick pounced on the rubber and drilled it
high and hard at McNeil. Almost miraculously, it wound up in
the Montreal net. Leswick's stunning goal gave the Red Wings
the Stanley Cup.

Later, Montreal's great defenseman Doug Harvey blamed himself for Leswick's winning goal. "I was in front of Leswick when
he shot," said Harvey. "I reached up for the puck, intending to
knock it away. But the damn puck struck my glove and caromed
in past McNeil."

The Red Wings — least of all Tony Leswick — didn't care how the puck went in. They'd won the game and all the laurels. Leswick was mobbed by his mates. Fans leaped over the boards and onto the ice. There was a long delay while the ice was cleared for the Cup presentation. NHL president Clarence Campbell turned the Stanley Cup over to Marguerite Norris, the team president, and to a beaming Jack Adams, the general manager.

By then the Montreal players had left the ice. None of them stayed around to congratulate the winners and they were roundly criticized for their poor sportsmanship by the Detroit media.

Tony Leswick would play a couple more seasons in the NHL, and enjoy many other satisfying moments. But none so much as the shot that lit the light behind Gerry McNeil on that muggy night of April 16, 1954, to bring the Cup to Detroit for the sixth time in Red Wing history.

Substitute Goalie Turns Net Around

BACK in the 1950s, NHL teams were not required to dress a backup goalie. Consequently, when a goalie was injured in a game and could not return, some surprising events took place on the ice. Consider the case of Ross "Lefty" Wilson, assistant trainer and practice goalie for the Detroit Red Wings.

Lefty — "only my mother calls me Ross" — played junior hockey in Toronto, then was recruited during the war to play for the Toronto Navy team. He was a capable puckstopper and his team once captured the All-Ontario intermediate championship.

In the fall of 1944, Jack Adams signed Lefty and sent him to Omaha, where he would not only play goal but serve as the assistant trainer. Adams soon discovered that young Wilson was hardly the reincarnation of Georges Vezina. "As a goaltender," he told his associates, "the kid makes a pretty good trainer." Lefty himself recalls, "I didn't know much about either job but I took them both." In Omaha, he was a teammate of a teenaged Gordie Howe and was tutored by Tommy Ivan, who would one day coach the Red Wings.

In time, Wilson was promoted to the Red Wings as the practice goalie and assistant trainer. One of his duties, of course, was to be available as an emergency replacement. Lefty soon became renowned as "the noisiest man in the NHL." From behind the Detroit bench he could often be heard heckling the referees and opponents. He also shouted encouragement to the Red Wing players and often turned toward the seats to exchange insults with spectators. One year, Lefty was reprimanded by the NHL after a complaint from Conn Smythe, who accused him of using abusive language against the referee as well as the Leafs.

Lefty did get a few chances to strap on the pads in league action. On October 10, 1953, he replaced the Wings' Terry Sawchuk, who'd limped off the ice with a split kneecap. The portly Wilson played 10 minutes of shutout hockey for Detroit.

There was always the risk he'd have to suit up against his mates in a game, and that happened at the Olympia on January 22, 1956, when Lefty was called upon to replace Harry Lumley of the Leafs. It was no secret the Leafs were Lefty's least favorite team. Now he was obliged to leave the friendly surroundings of the Red Wing bench, suit up, and try to thwart his own team for the final 13 minutes and 9 seconds of the match.

The Maple Leafs, trailing 4–1 when Lefty shuffled onto the ice, began to check fiercely for the newcomer in goal. And Wilson appreciated it. He began to encourage the Leafs with shouts that could be heard throughout the arena.

According to one newspaper report of the game, Lumley was "replaced by a comedian, the trainer Wilson who convulsed 13,861 fans with his histrionics until the finish. The fans cheered his every stop and laughed hilariously at his screams of encouragement to the Leafs. Lefty had the crowd in stitches with his jumping jack antics and running fire of advice."

Lefty was determined to use any means to keep Howe, Lindsay, and the other Wings from scoring, if only to earn bragging rights back in the Detroit dressing room. On one rush, as the Wings swarmed up the ice toward him, he lifted the net off its moorings and turned it around. Then he waved his stick frantically at the referee, howling for a stop in play! And he got one, of course. It was an "accident," he said lamely.

Lefty kept his shutout string alive by stopping Gordie Howe on two difficult shots. He kept the Olympia faithful in an uproar by frustrating the very team that was paying his salary.

Lefty Wilson donned the pads one more time two seasons later, replacing Don Simmons in the Boston goal. He then "retired" to concentrate on his training chores, which he handled until 1982. His goaltending stats are quite remarkable. He allowed just one goal in 85 minutes of play, for a goals-against average of 0.71. And he's the answer to a great trivia question: Name the only player who played three games in the NHL — with three different teams.

Letting Three Great Goalies Go

I N the six-team league of the 1950s the Detroit Red Wings displayed an uncanny ability to discover and develop star goalies. At different times in the decade the Wings employed Harry Lumley, Terry Sawchuk, and Glenn Hall. All three are now honored members of the Hockey Hall of Fame.

Jack Adams also made a habit of trading each of his stellar netminders while they still appeared to be in their prime. Both Lumley and Sawchuk had just won Stanley Cups for Detroit the year before they were traded. In 1950, Adams sent Lumley, along with Pete Babando (whose overtime goal had won the Stanley

Cup for Detroit three months earlier), Jack Stewart, Al Dewsbury, and Don Morrison to Chicago in return for goalie Jim Henry, Bob Goldham, Gaye Stewart, and Metro Prystai. It was called the biggest trade in NHL history. Once he dumped Lumley, who was only 24, Adams promoted Terry Sawchuk from the Red Wings' Indianapolis farm club. Sawchuk led the NHL in shutouts in his rookie season and won the Calder Trophy as the NHL's top rookie.

If Sawchuk felt his splendid play meant job security he was kidding himself. In 1955, in another multi-player deal, Adams dispatched the 25-year-old Sawchuk to Boston along with Marcel Bonin, Vic Stasiuk, and Lorne Davis, in return for Real Chevrefils, Ed Sandford, Warren Godfrey, Gilles Boisvert, and Norm Corcoran.

Adams could afford to trade a goalie who was already being acclaimed as one of the best ever, because there was someone just as good waiting in the wings. In two of his previous three seasons, a youngster by the name of Glenn Hall had played in eight games, filling in for an injured Sawchuk, winning all but two. Adams felt that Hall was not only ready to star in the NHL but that he had the talent to become one of the all-time greats. On both counts he would be proven correct.

Although he did not win a Stanley Cup with Detroit, Glenn Hall played exceptionally well. But his best years were still ahead of him — with Chicago, where he would backstop some powerful Blackhawk teams to one Stanley Cup and two other trips to the finals. "Mr. Goalie," as he would become known, was traded from the Wings after only two full seasons to accommodate the return of Sawchuk to Adams's fold. Sawchuk had quit the Bruins and gone into hiding after a dispute with Boston management and after the Boston papers goaded him to the point where he threatened to sue.

Adams liked Hall but he liked Sawchuk better. He gave up Johnny Bucyk — who went on to a brilliant, lengthy career as a Bruin — and cash for Sawchuk, and dealt Hall to Chicago with Ted Lindsay in return for goalie Hank Bassen, Forbes Kennedy, Bill Preston, and Johnny Wilson.

Adams must have been pleased as he watched the All-Star Game of 1955. Glenn Hall was in goal for his Wings while Terry Sawchuk shared the All-Star netminding duties with Harry Lumley. The Detroit farm system had supplied all three.

The trading of three great goalies — in their prime — would be unheard of today. But Adams loved making deals, shaking up his roster. And you can't argue with success. Adams's Detroit teams of the '50s were indeed among the greatest ever assembled, with four Stanley Cups.

Johnny Wilson Looks Back

J OHNNY Wilson played left wing on four Stanley Cup–winning Detroit teams between 1950 and 1955, and at one time was the NHL's all-time iron man, playing in 580 consecutive games. He recalls the aftermath of one of the Cup wins being the genesis of an ill-fated player revolt.

"In those days the players got a $3,000 bonus from the league for winning the Cup. Of that amount about $500 went to the IRS so we wound up with about $2,600. Well, we got our bonus money one year and it amounted to only $1,900. That puzzled us, especially Ted Lindsay. So Teddy called a meeting of the players and he said, 'I want to know what happened to the other six hundred.' He went to Jack Adams and you know what Adams said to him? He said, 'Look, the 17 players aren't the only ones who should get a share of this bonus money.'

"Lindsay said, 'Yeah, the trainer gets a share, the coach gets a share, and the assistant trainer gets half a share. Who else should get a share?'

"Ted found out that Adams had given shares or partial shares to the box office manager, the scouts, the head electrician, the public-relations director — everybody. There were 29 people in the organization who shared in the playoff money and that wasn't right. Why should Jack Adams be giving our money to everybody in the organization?

"That's when Teddy started thinking seriously about starting a players' association. When it came to money, Jack would knock us down, knock us down. I don't know why. And Ted got so mad about it he went over Jack's head one year and signed his next contract with the Norris brothers because he felt he was worth a lot more money than Jack would pay him. And Ted was right. He was always in the running for the scoring title, on the All-Star team, a great leader."

Wilson remembers when future Hall of Fame goalie Glenn Hall joined the Wings. "We were playing in the Montreal Forum and [Terry] Sawchuk was hurt. So they flew Glenn Hall in from Edmonton to play in his first NHL game.

"Now the Forum dressing room was kinda small. Everything was in one area — the showers, the john, everything. So there's not any privacy.

"Poor old Glenn is suiting up, getting ready to face the Rocket, Geoffrion, Beliveau — all those great Montreal players. And is he nervous! Who wouldn't be? Now he bolts for the toilet and starts to throw up. He's barfing in there and you could hear him a mile away. We start laughing and Gordie and the guys are yelling, 'Way to go, Glenn, get all that stuff up. We don't want you doing that out on the ice.'

He comes out of the john and his face is as white as a sheet. And we're all thinking, 'Geez, what kind of a game is this kid going to play?' Well, if memory serves he played a helluva game and I believe we beat the Canadiens 2–1 that night."

Wilson coached the Red Wings for a couple of seasons in the early '70s and he is asked which coach had the greatest effect on him. He says, "When I was traded to Chicago I had Dick Irvin as my coach and he was quite a gentleman. We had training camp at the old rink in Welland one year and Dick was disturbed when he looked over the record of the team after a couple of exhibition games. We hadn't scored any goals and we'd given up quite a few.

"So we're in the dressing room one day when Dick drags in a goal net. In this small space the net looks as big as a soccer goal. He holds up a hockey puck and he says, 'You mean you fellows can't put a tiny hockey puck into this big net. That's unbelievable!' He made it appear to be the easiest thing in the world.

"Another time he called us into the dressing room and he had the chairs lined up like a classroom. Then he had someone pass pencils and paper all around. 'Gentlemen, today we're going to have a little quiz,' he said. 'I'd like to test your knowledge of the game of hockey. First question. How big is the puck?'

"Nobody puts his pencil to the paper. Dick waits while 20 players fidget and frown and try to peek over the shoulder of the guy ahead of him. Nobody seems to know the answer to the question so he moves on.

"'Question number two. What's the maximum length of a hockey stick?' Again we hem and haw and guys are just guessing at the answer.

"After a couple of more questions with no better results, Dick gives it up. He says in disgust, 'You men shouldn't be playing hockey for a living. You should be back in school.'"

Red Wings Benefit
from Forum Riot

WHEN Montreal's Rocket Richard was suspended for assaulting a game official during the last week of the 1954–55 season, the Detroit Red Wings were the beneficiaries. They won both a league championship and a Stanley Cup that might otherwise have gone to Montreal.

You probably know the story of the infamous St. Patrick's Day riot of 1955. NHL president Clarence Campbell suspended Richard for his attack on Boston Bruin defenseman Hal Laycoe and for striking linesman Cliff Thompson during a melee at the Boston Garden. Since the regular season was nearly over, the suspension included all playoff games that spring. Montrealers, particularly francophones, were incensed over the severity of the punishment and they cursed Campbell. The next game at the Forum, on the night of March 17, against Detroit, was never finished.

The story of that game has been told and retold. The fans were in an ugly mood and their demeanor worsened when the Red Wings slapped in four fast goals in the first period. The Canadiens, tied in the standings prior to the game, could see their hold on the league championship slipping away. Richard, standing in the shadows that night, could see his chance at a scoring crown (a title he desperately wanted to win but never had, and never would) was in jeopardy as well.

Campbell arrived late for the game, accompanied by his secretary. As they took their seats, the league president was assailed with taunts and slurs from the crowd, which had been stirred up by press coverage of the suspension. A hoodlum approached Campbell and held out his hand, as if to offer a friendly greeting. Then he quickly made a fist and punched Campbell. Other thugs joined in; one of them squeezed a tomato on Campbell's head. Garbage and eggs rained down from above.

Police rushed to the scene and rescued the president. As they were leading him to safety a tear-gas bomb exploded on the ice and people began coughing and choking from the fumes. The Forum was in an uproar. People ran for the exits, but luckily there was no real panic. The game was halted, and eventually forfeited to the Wings.

Outside the Forum a mob gathered. Vandals threw rocks at the Forum walls and windows, then surged down Ste. Catherine Street smashing windows, looting, and setting fires. Damage would later be estimated at $100,000.

The forfeited game added two points to Detroit's total and, when the Red Wings beat Montreal in the final game of the season a few nights later, they captured the league title — by two points — for a seventh consecutive season.

Rocket Richard was deprived of his dream of a scoring crown when teammate Boom Boom Geoffrion edged him out by one point, 75–74. Both players tallied 38 goals. But there was no glory for Geoffrion, who was scorned by Canadiens fans who felt the title should have belonged to the Rocket. Under any other circumstances, these same fans would have applauded Boom Boom's achievement.

As fate would have it, Detroit and Montreal met in the finals, and the series went the full seven games. Alex Delvecchio scored a pair of goals in Detroit's 3–1 seventh-game victory at the Olympia to keep the Cup in Detroit. All seven games in the series were won by the home team, so it could be suggested the Richard suspension lost Montreal the Cup.

After the traditional backslaps and embraces, the Wings were surprised to see the Canadiens skate over to offer their congratulations. After Detroit's Cup victory a year earlier, the Habs had stormed off to their dressing room.

President Campbell presented the Stanley Cup to Red Wings president Marguerite Norris, the first woman to have her name engraved on the Cup. Team captain Ted Lindsay made a brief speech and the team went off to celebrate.

Today, no Stanley Cup win would be complete without the awarding of Stanley Cup rings. In those days, "Forget it. We never got rings," says Marcel Pronovost, a trace of bitterness in his voice almost 45 years later.

Glenn Hall Says . . .

"**I**N my day, as a goaltender, you pretty much learned on your own. But you had to learn if you wanted to make it to the NHL. And even though I played only a couple of years with the Red Wings, I was in their system for ten years. There were two years in junior at Windsor, a year and a half in Humboldt, four years with their minor-league clubs, and then the two in Detroit with the Wings.

"People kid me about throwing up before the games and being so nervous, but I was always ready to play. Always. My strength was in my skating although I had quick reflexes and good balance, too. The idea then was to get your feet in the puck's way and your head out of it. Goalies couldn't afford the luxury of getting a puck in the face or head — not without a face mask.

"I avoided training camp whenever I could. Said I was painting the barn or something like that. I never thought training camp was necessary — not for me. There's no learning at training camp. I didn't think I had to be there just so some other fellows could get in shape. So when I didn't report to training camp and the phone would ring and someone wanted to know where I was, I'd tell my wife, Pauline, 'Tell them I haven't finished painting the barn.'

"Goalies are generally loners. At least they were in my day. But I enjoyed being alone. Just like I enjoy open spaces. I get stuck in a city too long and I yearn to head for the hills. I guess it would have been nice to have someone to talk to when I broke in. But when I signed with Detroit, Terry Sawchuk and Harry Lumley were the goalies. If they knew anything about stopping pucks — and I can't begin to guess who knew more — they certainly weren't going to pass that information along. They knew what I had in mind — taking away their job! There was no reason for them to tell me anything. Goalies didn't do those things then. Heck, there were only six or eight goalies in the entire NHL. It was tough to hang onto a job."

Dineen Rewarded by Jolly Jack

BILL Dineen was an Ottawa boy who graduated from Toronto's St. Michael's College to join the Red Wings for the 1953–54 season. He enjoyed an excellent rookie season, scoring 17 goals, although his achievements would understandably be overlooked on a team that boasted four of the league's top seven scorers — Gordie Howe (first), Ted Lindsay (third), Red Kelly (sixth), and Dutch Reibel (seventh).

Detroit placed first for the fifth year in a row, then captured the Stanley Cup in a thrilling seven-game series with Montreal.

Dineen couldn't believe his good fortune. He'd broken in with one of the greatest teams ever assembled, and played on a Cup winner right out of the box. And his 17 goals, he'd been told, were an important contribution to the team's success.

Now it came time to discuss his future with the Red Wings. In a meeting with GM Jack Adams, Bill suggested that a raise might be in order in light of all the good things that had happened.

"How much are we paying you now?" Adams asked the shy winger.

"I signed for $6,000," Dineen replied.

"And you want a raise, do you? How much do you have in mind?" Adams asked.

"Well, I was thinking $500, but . . ."

"Say no more, young man. You've got your raise. You've earned it." Adams smiled and shook Dineen's hand.

Some time later, after talking with the other Red Wings, Dineen discovered why Jack Adams had been so agreeable about the raise. In the off-season, the NHL had set its minimum salary at $6500. Dineen's raise would have happened anyway. But Jack Adams never missed an opportunity to play the role of the benevolent manager.

Dineen's 17 goals turned out to be his career high. But he contibuted to the NHL in other ways. His three sons, Peter, Gord, and Kevin, played in the NHL, while Bill went on to coach the Philadelphia Flyers between 1991 and 1993.

Adams Picks His Best

NO other team, not even the Montreal dynasty of the late '50s, has ever matched Detroit's run of seven consecutive first-place finishes from in the NHL standings from 1948–49 through 1954–55. A decade after the Wings' reign ended, manager Jack Adams was asked to name the players who contributed the most at each position during the seven-year stretch.

Without hesitating he put the famed Production Line at the top of his list. "Sure they were the best," he said. "Sid Abel at center, Gordie Howe on right wing, and Ted Lindsay on the left side. The greatest line ever, no matter what they say in Montreal. Then I'd choose Red Kelly and Bob Goldham as my defensemen — and don't tell me I've overlooked two great ones in Bill Quackenbush and Jack Stewart. Each was a marvel in his time but Quackenbush played in only one of the seasons we're talking about and Stewart played in two. Goldham contributed gilt-edged hockey for five of those years. In goal, who else but Terry Sawchuk."

Lindsay a Detroit Fixture

TERRIBLE Ted Lindsay will be forever known as one of the best left wingers in hockey. With Lindsay's help, the Red Wings powered their way to eight regular-season titles and four Stanley Cups in the late 1940s and early 1950s.

Despite his small stature (five foot eight, 160 pounds), no opponent was too big or too tough for Lindsay. When provoked he was fearless and ferocious. One sportswriter of his era wrote,

"Hockey's most spectacular bloodlettings have usually involved Lindsay." In 1952, Tim Cohane of *Look* magazine called him "a picture of unmitigated villainy."

His boss, Jack Adams, said, "I've never seen a better left winger. And that goes for Aurel Joliat or any of the rest of them. When he goes out on the ice, nobody is his friend. He'd be a great guy to throw into a game in which there were no rules." Those words of admission were spoken early in Lindsay's career. There would come a time when Adams would spit rather than mention the left winger's name.

Marty Pavelich, a teammate and business partner of Lindsay's for many years, says, "Teddy took a lot of riding from a lot of people. It only made him play better hockey. Ted never backed down. He didn't even complain when Rocket Richard knocked him cold with a sucker punch in the '51 playoffs. Don't think Richard didn't suffer some lumps in return somewhere down the road for that. And Bill Ezinicki! Now there was a tough character, but not too tough for Lindsay."

Pavelich was referring to an epic battle between Lindsay and Ezinicki that erupted at the Olympia on January 25, 1951. Lindsay caught Ezinicki with a punch that sent the Bruin crashing to the ice. Tim Cohane decribed what happened next. "Lindsay leaped on him like a jaguar and was pummeling him before he realized Ezinicki was unconscious from his fall." Ezinicki required 19 stitches and lost a tooth. Both players were suspended for three Boston–Detroit games and fined $200.

For years, Lindsay was the all-time penalty leader in the NHL. His records have since been eclipsed by such modern-day enforcers as Tiger Williams, Dale Hunter, and Marty McSorley.

Former referee Red Storey recalls Lindsay as being a "last-word kind of guy," someone who often gave verbal critiques of an official's work, and seldom were they complimentary.

"He snarled something almost loud enough for me to hear one night," says Storey, laughing at the memory. "I yelled over, 'What did you say, Lindsay? I can't hear you.' And he put a hand over his eyes and yelled back, 'Red, you can't see me, either.' Now that was a snappy comeback."

Adams and Lindsay had a falling out when Adams discovered Lindsay and Pavelich were business partners outside of hockey. The two were involved in a company supplying plastics to the auto industry. "When Jack heard about that, his attitude toward us changed completely," Lindsay recalls. "It was as if he saw us as traitors." Adams was further steamed when he discovered that Lindsay was the ringleader of a fledgling players' association. That was in 1957. Despite his 30 goals and 85 points, good for second place (to Gordie Howe) in the scoring race, Lindsay was traded to the last-place Chicago Blackhawks. It was Adams's way of saying, "Anyone who likes a union can like it in Chicago," in those days the hockey equivalent of Siberia.

Adams was so intent on making Lindsay out to be an ingrate that he drew up and showed reporters a fake contract that indicated Lindsay was earning $25,000 as a Red Wing. In reality, Lindsay was paid about $12,000 a year.

Lindsay retired from hockey after the 1959–60 season, but four years later, at age 39, he made a remarkable comeback with Detroit. NHL president Clarence Campbell thought Lindsay's comeback attempt was farcical, and when Terrible Ted became involved in several spats and tiffs with league officials, Campbell summoned the firebrand to his office. But Lindsay refused to attend, and openly mocked Campbell's "kangaroo court." He was fined $75 and ordered to submit a written apology. With 14 goals and 14 assists, Lindsay declared his comeback a success and most fans agreed with him.

Ted Lindsay was general manager of the Red Wings from 1977 to 1980 and, perhaps recalling Adams's stinginess, he paid his players handsomely. When I worked with Ted on the NBC telecasts in the mid '70s his strong opinions were a feature of every show. In 1995 he was employed as a consultant and an interview subject on a fascinating CBC documentary, *Net Worth*, which listed many of hockey's ills, including the power wielded over players by men like his former boss, Jack Adams.

He works out every day, still skates with power and poise and faces his forthcoming 75th birthday with a shrug. When he blows out the candles on that cake, a layer of icing may fly off and hit the wall.

5

Gordie Leads the Way

The Goal Gadsby
Can't Forget

DEFENSEMAN Bill Gadsby was one of the unluckiest guys in hockey. He played the first 15 years of his career with Chicago and New York, teams that made the playoffs a combined four times from 1946 to 1961.

Then in 1961–62, Gadbsy was traded by New York to Detroit (for Les Hunt, who never played an NHL game) where he at last experienced the joys of winning. The Red Wings made it to the Cup finals in three of Gadsby's five seasons in the red and white. Surely now he would get to taste champagne from Lord Stanley's old basin.

But it was not to be. Toronto swept the Wings aside in five games in the 1963 finals. In 1964, the Leafs required seven games to capture their third consecutive Cup. Leaf defenseman Bobby Baun scored in overtime in game six, a turning point. Baun was given hero status for winning the game while reportedly playing on a broken leg.

"Bah," says Gadsby, "his leg wasn't broken. He may have had a hairline fracture but the media played it up big. I remember skating up to Baun before game seven. I said, 'Who do you think you're kidding?' He just kind of shrugged."

The following season, 1964–65, The Blackhawks ousted the Wings in seven games in the semifinals. "Bobby Hull and Glenn Hall did us in that year," recalls Gadsby. "By then I was almost 38 years old and running out of time.

"In the '66 playoffs we turned the tables on the Hawks and ousted them in six games. That put us into the finals against

Montreal. The Habs were huge favorites, mind you, because we'd finished something like 16 points behind them during the regular season. We played the first two games at the Forum and Roger Crozier, our little goalie, just stoned them. He was sensational and we won the first two games.

"I really thought we had them. But the Habs stormed back and won the next two back on our ice. They won again in Montreal and now we're back at home for game six. Suddenly we're hot again and we're tied with the Canadiens after regulation time.

"The overtime period was a couple of minutes old when Henri Richard flew in on Crozier. Somehow he fell down and went sliding toward the goal and Crozier. Just then the puck came to him and he slid with it into the net. He shoved the damn thing in with his arm — I know he did. But the red light flashed, and the Habs began jumping on the ice. I looked at the referee, John Ashley, and he just stood there. He didn't wave it off. The series was over and I can't believe it ended like it did.

"After all these years, I still say Ashley should never have allowed that goal. It was a lousy way for us to lose. I knew right then I'd probably never get another chance at the Cup."

Long after the series was over, Montreal coach Toe Blake confessed that he too thought the Richard goal would be called back, so he ordered his players to leap on the ice immediately and start celebrating. He didn't want to give the referee time to think about the legitimacy of the goal, or to confer with anyone else.

To the Habs, the Cup win was old hat. It was their seventh in the past 11 years. But to Gadsby, it was a tragedy, the end of a dream.

It should be noted that it wasn't John Ashley who refereed the playoff game that Gadsby can't forget: it was Frank Udvari. Udvari once said, "Balon shot the puck and it hit Henri Richard on the arm or the shoulder and he slid into Crozier on his stomach. I called it a goal."

John Ferguson, watching from the Montreal bench, remembers it this way: "Richard kept sliding and sliding and sliding at Crozier until he slid right into the net, with the puck and Crozier. The goal judge had no choice but to hit the red light because the puck had crossed the line. Meanwhile, Toe Blake was watching the whole thing and the minute the red light flashed he yelled down the bench, 'Get out on the ice! Get out there!' So we tumbled over the boards and headed for Richard. Toe figured if we jumped on the ice and made it appear that everything about the goal was legit, maybe Udvari would swallow his whistle. And Toe was exactly right. Udvari seemed stunned and did nothing to wave off the goal. The Red Wings were in a trance as well and by then we knew the goal was going to count and we could start whooping it up in earnest."

Gadsby's 20-year quest for a Stanley Cup went unfulfilled. But he can count himself fortunate for even having had a career in the NHL after surviving two terrifying traumas early in his life. First was during an ocean crossing on the *Athenia* during the war. The ship was torpedoed and 12-year-old Gadsby was rescued after spending several hours in a lifeboat. Later, when he was 25, he came down with polio in an era when thousands of young people were crippled by the disease. Gadbsy was lucky enough to recover and pursue a career in hockey.

Smarten Up, Baun Tells Howe

D EFENSEMAN Bobby Baun had played 11 years with Toronto and one with the Oakland Seals before he joined the Detroit Red Wings for the 1969–70 season. In those days, players' salaries were seldom discussed — the teams wanted it that way and some of the players did, too — perhaps because they were embarrassed to reveal how little they were earning.

Baun went against the grain. He always gave the appearance of being well heeled, even in junior hockey when he'd flash a fat roll of bills and drive a bigger, faster car than the other teenage stars.

In his second season as a Red Wing, Baun invited Gordie Howe to lunch. This was during training camp in Port Huron, Michigan. Baun came right to the point: "Gordie, you old fart, when are you going to smarten up?"

"What do you mean by that?" Gordie answered, almost spilling his drink.

"Listen to me," said Baun. "I want you to know something. You've got the biggest name in hockey and I'm making twice as much money as you are. What do you think of that?"

Howe gulped. He couldn't believe it. He'd been assured for years that he was the highest-paid Red Wing.

"How much are you making?" Howe asked.

"Ninety grand a year," Baun said without missing a beat. "Double what you're getting."

Baun added to Howe's discomfort by adding, "If that isn't hard enough to swallow, how about this: Carl Brewer is making more money than both of us."

The next day Gordie marched into the Red Wings' front office and demanded a renegotiation of his contract. Owner Bruce Norris, embarrassed to have been caught deceiving the Red Wings' greatest asset, quickly agreed. Howe's salary was more than doubled. But a rift in Gordie's relationship with the owner had been created, one that would never heal.

Norris couldn't resist taking a verbal shot at the Howes as Gordie left his office: "Well, I hope that'll make Colleen happy," he snorted.

Playing the Pest Position

HOW is a forward able to play 16 seasons in the NHL with six different clubs, average just one goal per season — and still keep his job?

It's easy if your name is Bryan "Bugsy" Watson.

Watson, a Detroit favorite for most of five seasons, was hockey's premier pest, a pugnacious little guy, a shit disturber of the first degree. He displayed an amazing ability to drive opponents to distraction with his tricky play and his in-your-face approach to the game.

"Nobody could get under your skin like that little so-and-so," Leaf manager Punch Imlach once said. "No wonder they nicknamed him Bugsy. "In the '60s he drove most of the best players in the game absolutely crazy."

Bobby Hull agrees. During the 1965–66 season, Chicago's Golden Jet reached superstardom by scoring 54 goals, shattering Rocket Richard's 21-year-old standard of 50. When the Blackhawks met the Red Wings in the 1966 semifinals, the Wings had to find a way to stop Hull.

"Hell, I can do that," Watson said confidently, even though Hull outweighed him by 20 pounds and was so strong he could have picked Watson up by the scruff of the neck and dropped him off in the penalty box — which, incidentally, was Watson's second home.

Detroit coach Sid Abel knew Bugsy was the perfect man for the job. He knew Watson would stick to Hull like gum to shoe leather.

Throughout the series, which lasted six games, Watson made Hull's hockey life miserable, following him maniacally and goading Hull into some stupid penalties. "The secret was to shadow him but not get him too mad," Watson recalled. "I didn't want him to get so angry he'd go crazy and score goals all over the place." Sid Abel said with a grin, "It looked to me like they were chained together out there. Watson was a big reason we won the series four games to two. I thought he was going to follow Hull into the showers when it was over."

"Boy, did he bug me," snapped Hull, who'd never been so thoroughly shadowed in his career.

"That was my role in hockey," Watson said. "If I could have scored like Hull, do you think I'd have been such a pest? When you score 17 goals in 16 seasons you'd better have something else to offer. I used every trick I knew to get the opposing team — and its best players — stirred up. I could often foul an opponent like Hull and get away with it. An elbow, a crosscheck, a sneaky little trip, interfere with the guy — if you're slick you can pull it off and not get a penalty."

Not that Watson's many sly fouls in his career went undetected. At one time he led all NHL players in penalty minutes and served over 2,000 minutes in the box — an average of nearly three minutes per game.

Watson learned how to dish it out from one of hockey's most feared competitors, Montreal Canadiens' enforcer John Ferguson. Early in their careers, they were roommates with the Habs. Ferguson had quickly established a reputation as hockey's heavyweight champ while Watson had aspirations to hold the middleweight title.

Ferguson says, "That Bugsy. Pound for pound he was the toughest kid in hockey. He took an awful lot of punishment from some of the biggest guys in the game. But he never quit, never backed off. Everyone in the NHL admired his tenacity."

Watson's battered mug, with its dented nose and its multitude of scars, reveals the kind of player he was. Hockey writer Frank Orr once described his face as looking like "a bagful of doorknobs."

"If you hand it out, you'd better be prepared to take it," Watson says. "That's the way it's always been in the NHL."

Today, at age 55, Watson spends a lot of time working with the Special Olympics. Fans who remember him as a bundle of fury on the ice are amazed at the softer, gentler side he displays when he's among the handicapped. "His commitment to the handicapped and the less fortunate is truly amazing," says Frank Selke,

Jr., who was an executive with the Canadiens when Watson first joined the NHL.

"Here's a personal anecdote," says Selke. "My son Gary was nine when he was hospitalized with rheumatic fever. I put a note on the dressing room wall asking the Montreal players, if they had time, to visit Gary. The only one who did was Bryan Watson. And he came every day to talk with Gary, to help him with his homework. And he signed countless autographs for all the other kids in the ward. Gary is in his forties now and he still thinks Bryan Watson is one of the greatest individuals he's ever met."

Faulkner First Newfie to Score

IMAGINE receiving a telegram signed by 4,000 well-wishers, along with numerous letters and cards, prior to your first game as a Red Wing. That's the kind of support Alex Faulkner was given when he joined Detroit prior to the 1962–63 season. Faulkner had played one game as a Toronto Maple Leaf the season before, and the fans in his native Newfoundland immediately placed him on a pedestal. He was the first from that province to make the NHL.

Faulkner was determined not to let them down, and in his third game as a Red Wing, playing against Jacques Plante and the Montreal Canadiens, he potted his first NHL goal, the first ever by a player from the "Rock."

The Cheerleader

I N the late 1960s, rugged centerman Pete Stemkowski enjoyed two good seasons in a Detroit uniform. He might have stayed around much longer if it hadn't been for his rebellious nature.

The end came for Stemmer when new coach Ned Harkness joined the club in 1970, resulting in a clash of personalities. Stemkowski was known for his relaxed, fun-loving approach to the game while Harkness prided himself on being a stern disciplinarian.

Stemkowski recalls two incidents that he feels led to his departure from Detroit in a trade to the New York Rangers.

"You know, when Harkness came along we had a bunch of old pros on the Red Wings, guys like Gordie and Alex Delvecchio and Gary Bergman and myself. Frankly we didn't know what to make of Harkness. He was a rah-rah college guy and the first thing he did was order us to wear blue blazers and gray slacks and to butt out our cigars. Geez, that last rule was a blow to Alex because he's had a cigar in his mouth since the day he was born. I remember Tommy Webster's wife had a baby that year, and when Tommy passed out the traditional cigars, Ned barked at the guys, 'Put those cigars in your pockets or in the garbage can — but don't smoke them!'

"So we made a few comments about the guy behind his back and one day he was late for a morning practice. I was goofing around in the dressing room and for some reason I stood up and played the role of a cheerleader. 'Gimme a C!' I yelled. 'Gimme an O, gimme an R, gimme an N . . .' But before I could spell out C-O-R-N-E-L-L, I realized the guys had stopped responding. After the first couple of letters they'd hushed up. I soon found out why. Ned Harkness had slipped into the room and was standing right behind me. Talk about mocking someone and being caught redhanded. That was me. I knew right then that my stay in Detroit was probably not going to be a long one.

"Bobby Baun, my roomie at the time, loves to tell this story. We played an exhibition game in Port Huron one night. I was single at the time so I invited a great-looking girl I knew to come up and see the game. It was just an exhibition game and I didn't figure Ned would lay on a blinkin' curfew afterwards. But he did, telling us, 'One o'clock curfew, men. No ifs, ands, or buts.'

"So I meet this girl after the game and already it's about 11:30 p.m. We have a couple of drinks and it's obvious she's a little amorous so we take a walk on the beach. This is in September and it's cold out. We drop down in the sand and roll around a bit but I say, 'This won't do. This is ridiculous. Come on back to my room.'

"She says, 'What about your roommate?'

"I say, 'I'm rooming with Bobby Baun. There won't be a problem. The guy sleeps like a log. Once he hits the sack, nothing will wake him up.'

"So we hurry back to the hotel and now I've missed curfew by about fifteen minutes. Figure I better sneak up the back stairs. I tell the girl, 'You follow along. I'll make sure the coast is clear.'

"I get up to my floor and who the hell is standing there but Ned Harkness. His room is just a couple of doors away from mine. He says, 'Come on in for a minute.' So I say, 'Sure' and I go in his room. What else could I do? He says, 'You've got sand on your clothes.' I look surprised and say, 'Geez, how'd that get there?'

"He says, 'Great game tonight.' I say, 'Thanks. We're coming along. We'll be all right.' He looks at his watch and says, 'You know, you've missed curfew by a few minutes.' I say, 'Did I? Geez, the guys were all getting food at the take-out counter around the corner. My food arrived a little later than the others.' I thought it was a good excuse. He didn't seem to notice that I wasn't carrying any food.

"So he smiles and says, 'That's okay. Get a good night's sleep. I'll see you tomorrow.'

"He throws open the door to let me out and guess who's standing there, brushing sand off her skirt? She grins and says, 'Hi Pete. Can I come in now?'

"There was no way I could talk my way out of that situation. Ned slapped me with a fine and sure enough, it wasn't long before I got a phone call.

At first I was disappointed but everything turned out swell for me as a Ranger. Had half a dozen good years, met my wife there, bought a house, had some kids. Found a career in broadcasting after hockey. New York turned out to be a good move for me.

"I suppose I've got Ned Harkness to thank for that but I'm not really sure. You see, he told me once that it wasn't his idea to trade me, that Sid Abel was the one who insisted on the deal. But years later, I ran into Abel and he looked me right in the eye and said he wanted to keep me with the Wings, but that Ned Harkness was adamant that I be dealt. That's hockey for you."

Ullman Sets Playoff Record

NORM Ullman played pro hockey for 22 seasons and never won a Stanley Cup. But he set a Stanley Cup record that has never been broken — two goals in five seconds. And he scored them against one of the greatest netminders in history.

"We were playing Chicago in the 1965 playoffs," Ullman recalls, "and Glenn Hall was tending goal for the Blackhawks. He was always hard to beat. Late in the second period I took a shot from well out, maybe 40 to 50 feet. The puck skimmed along the ice, caught the goal post, and went in. Then, right off the face-off, I intercepted a pass and took another shot. This time [Chicago] defenseman Matt Ravlich screened Hall and another long shot found the net. I was amazed because all of this happened in just five seconds. The goals came at 17:35 and 17:40. Only later did I learn I'd set a record for the fastest two playoff goals. I don't think Glenn saw either shot. He didn't miss very many."

Ullman was a Red Wing for over 12 seasons and led the Wings in goals three times, twice in points. He was traded to Toronto a year after the Leafs won the '67 Stanley Cup. He scored 490 career goals and, as a Red Wing, was selected to play in eight All-Star Games. He was inducted into the Hockey Hall of Fame in 1982.

Detroit's Mr. Clean

ISN'T it odd that the NHL's *Official Guide and Record Book* lists the players who take the most penalties and completely overlooks those who take the fewest? There's Tiger Williams topping the career penalty list with 3,966 career minutes (4,421 including playoffs) and Dave "The Hammer" Schultz clinging to his 1975 record for most penalty minutes in one season — 472. That's equivalent to seven games in the sin bin out of an eighty-game schedule.

One former Red Wing of the '60s would qualify for the title of "cleanest player, least number of penalty minutes." During one stretch in his 13-year NHL career, he played in 185 consecutive games without being sent to the box. Later he managed to compile a streak of 157 penalty-free games.

His name was Val Fonteyne, a skinny little guy (five foot nine, 155 pounds) who excelled as a penalty killer in his Detroit days. And he avoided penalty boxes as if he was claustrophobic.

Playing in 820 NHL games, Fonteyne served all of 28 minutes in the penalty box. Compare that to Randy Holt of the Los Angeles Kings, who once drew 67 penalty minutes in one period! Fonteyne's the only player to complete three consecutive seasons without taking a single minor and the only one to compile five penalty-free seasons during his career. It shouldn't surprise us to learn he never served a major penalty for fighting — at least, not in the NHL. He vaguely recalls getting into a fight when he first turned pro with Seattle of the Western league.

Fans who like to ponder records, and long to see them broken, may have to wait for decades — perhaps forever — before someone as gentlemanly as Fonteyne breaks his records.

Baun's Broken-Ankle Shot Kills the Wings

IN 17 NHL seasons rugged defenseman Bob Baun scored only 37 times — about two goals per year. In close to 100 playoff games he scored only three times. One of those three, against Detroit in the 1964 Stanley Cup finals, turned out to be the biggest goal of his life. It's still talked about to this day.

Detroit led the series three games to two, and game six, at the Olympia, was tied 3–3. In the third period, Baun, a tough Maple Leaf rearguard, got in front of a Gordie Howe slapshot.

Baun crumpled in a heap when Howe's shot struck his ankle, and he had to be carried off the ice on a stretcher. The Red Wing medics examined Baun's leg and said they didn't think he could hurt it any more than he already had. Baun asked, "Can you freeze it?" and they said, "Sure."

Baun hobbled back on the ice for the overtime period. Early in the frame the puck came to him at the point. He shot it toward Detroit netminder Terry Sawchuk. He didn't expect to score. The puck flew right at defenseman Bill Gadsby, deflected off *his* stick, and lodged in the net behind Sawchuk. Game over.

Two days later, back at Maple Leaf Gardens, the Leafs blanked the Wings 4–0 and captured the Cup. Only then did Baun consent to X-rays on his damaged ankle. Sure enough, the bone was cracked.

Baun's broken-ankle goal has become a hockey legend. Unfortunately for the Red Wings, it was a goal that cost them the Stanley Cup.

The Bizarre Behavior
of Bruce Norris

WHEN Bruce Norris owned the Red Wings, he was known as a bully and a dictator. He could be boorish and insulting. He could be maudlin and sad. And if he was drinking, he could be capable of anything.

Colleen Howe admits she was often scared to death of him. So were many of the players, because he controlled their destinies.

One night at a party, after the Wings had been eliminated from the playoffs, Norris physically assaulted Parker MacDonald, one of his players.

At the time, MacDonald was going through a difficult time. His marriage was breaking up. He was depressed and couldn't sleep. And for some reason Bruce Norris took an intense dislike to him.

At the party, Norris approached MacDonald, who was standing behind a small bar. Norris offered his hand. When MacDonald took it, Norris, a big, strong man, pulled MacDonald sharply toward him. MacDonald's chest hit the edge of the bar and he dropped to the floor. Norris leaped on him, grabbed him by the throat, and began choking him. Bystanders were horrified. They couldn't believe their eyes. Here on the floor was the team owner throttling one of his players.

Wings' coach Bill Gadsby leaped up and ran to the writhing bodies. He grabbed Norris by the hands, bending his thumbs back, forcing his hands off MacDonald's throat. Norris staggered to his feet and was hustled out of the room. Witnesses said that Norris might easily have choked MacDonald to death if Gadsby hadn't intervened.

The story is one of the most interesting and shocking told by Gordie and Colleen Howe in their book *And . . . Howe.*

The Howes suggest wryly that the Norris–MacDonald confrontation led to the firing of Gadsby as coach of the Wings in 1969. Two games into the 1969–70 season, Norris told him what a great job he was doing. Less than two days later he fired him, and never explained why. Colleen Howe says, "Some people thought that Bruce Norris finally found out it was Gadsby who twisted his thumbs that night at the postseason party."

Another time, Gordie's teenage daughter Cathy was at a reception with her date one night when Bruce Norris came across the room. Obviously, he didn't recognize Cathy because he began to flirt with her. Cathy was astonished when this middle-aged man, her father's boss, tried to come on to her. When Norris mentioned he owned the Red Wings, Cathy delivered a zinger, "Then you must know my folks, Gordie and Colleen Howe." Norris almost fainted before beating a hasty retreat.

What a Comeback!

HE date was November 3, 1960, and the Red Wings were taking a beating on home ice from the lowly Boston Bruins. After two periods of play, the Bruins led 5–2.

General manager Jack Adams laced into his players during the second intermission and the pep talk led to the kind of comeback teams dream about. It started at 2:21 when Parker MacDonald scored for the Wings. At 4:45 Norm Ullman added another goal. Al Johnson tied the score three minutes later and, 44 seconds after that, Ullman scored again to put the Wings in front, 6–5. They tallied twice more to climax a six-goal outburst in a 12-minute span and nail down an 8–5 victory.

A Night for Pronovost

SPECIAL nights for hockey stars are not common occurrences in the NHL. In 1963, Red Wing defenseman Marcel Pronovost was so honored, but what was unusual was that it didn't take place at the Detroit Olympia.

Pronovost's big night was held in Montreal, at the Forum.

The good citizens of Beauharnois, Quebec, Pronovost's hometown, wanted to salute their native son. But, they couldn't afford to travel to Detroit for the ceremony. So they asked Frank Selke, general manager of the Montreal Canadiens, if they could honor Marcel during a Wings–Canadiens game at the Forum. "Why not?" replied Mr. Selke, although such a thing had never been done before. "I've always liked Marcel. Most of our fans admire him and wish he was a Montreal Canadien."

And a date was set.

Many of Marcel's boyhood friends, bursting with pride, were in the Forum for Marcel's night. Traditionally a new car is presented to the guest of honor on such an occasion, and the citizens of Beauharnois wanted very much to carry on this custom. They bought Marcel a lovely new car — the latest model. And they listened with pride to the huge ovation from the fans in the Forum when they turned over the keys to Marcel at center ice.

What wasn't publicized was that, to the embarrassment of the event organizers, Marcel's friends and neighbors had raised only half the price of the car. Of course, they couldn't present Pronovost with half a car! Someone took Marcel aside and asked if he would be interested in putting up the other half of the money for his "gift." If Marcel was shocked or offended, he hid it well.

"Sure," he said, always the good sport. "I'll buy half the car."

It was a wonderful night. And Mr. Selke even insisted that the ceremony be televised on the CBC, even though the TV producers told him they were running short on time.

To this day, few people know that Marcel Pronovost is the only hockey player honored with a night in another team's arena. Or that he paid for half of the shiny new car he received.

I asked Marcel, "Did they ever hold a night for you in Detroit?"

"Nope."

"Did you ever get Stanley Cup rings in Detroit?"

"Nope. Well, one year a nice man, a Mr. Higgins, gave us what they called Stanley Cup rings. He bought us rings with a red stone and wings on the side. And another time — it wasn't a Stanley Cup year — Mr. Norris gave us Rolex watches."

"What was your salary in 1952, the year you won the Cup in eight straight games?"

"I was making about $14,000. And I got an extra $2,700 for winning the Stanley Cup. I was shocked when I found out I was making more than Terry Sawchuk. And about the same as Gordie Howe."

"More than Lindsay?"

"Oh, no. Ted was a good negotiator. And later on, when he became manager, he paid his players well. He overpaid most of them."

Call It Twelve Foggy Years

W HEN he wasn't sitting in the penalty box he was sitting in a bar. Or in jail. When he wasn't starting a fight, he was finishing one. Or looking for another one. When he wasn't drunk, he was about to get drunk.

In the '60s, with his movie-star looks, he attracted women as successfully as Elvis. Over 60 now, he is still handsome and tanned, aging as gracefully as a Paul Newman or Robert Redford.

He is Howard John "Howie" Young, a muscular defenseman who joined the Red Wings in 1960–61. He broke hearts as easily as he broke hockey sticks, team rules, and curfews — and sometimes the law. He drove his bosses — and his teammates — wild with rage and frustration. "I'm through with the guy," Detroit manager Jack Adams snarled in 1962. NHL president Clarence Campbell followed up with, "He's the greatest detriment to hockey that has ever laced on skates."

There are many lingering images of his outrageous behavior on and off the ice. There was the time he showed up for a game wearing a Beatles wig. Then he shaved his head but for one strip down the middle. He once launched a shower of spit at Maple Leaf owner Stafford Smythe. He assaulted a cop and left him with a concussion. There are the times he was thrown in jail, beginning when he was in junior hockey, and the time he staggered drunkenly along the top rail of the boards at a Memorial Cup game, taunting coach Eddie Bush, and getting his picture in all the papers.

He was handsome, witty, and charming. His phone never stopped ringing. Teammate Marcel Pronovost says, "He was a devil to room with. He'd be out all night. The phone would ring at 2:00, at 4:00, again at 6:30. A woman would be crying, 'Where's Howie?' And when he'd stagger in, I'd say, 'Where the hell you been? Some woman is going to jump off a building if you don't call her.' He'd shrug and say, 'Nah, she won't.'"

In Detroit he was second to Howe in popularity — at least with the fans. He was the unpredictable kid with the crewcut, the big smile, the baby blue eyes — and a willingness to mix it up with the toughest hombres in hockey. His teammates were less patient with him than the fans. One year they lobbied to keep him out of the playoffs because they felt he hurt their chances.

It's amazing he was able to play as long and as well as he did, considering the vast quantities of booze he consumed and the fast lane he chose to run in. "Twelve foggy years," he told a reporter once. "Always drunk, always hungover. At games and practices I felt awful because I was hungover. And then there were all those guys on the ice who ran me, who wanted to take my head off. Stayin' sober is no big deal. Stayin' drunk is tough. That's what I worked at for a dozen years. Drinkin' and playin' hockey."

Between 1960 and 1971 the tough defenseman played five seasons with Detroit, two with Chicago, and one with the Vancouver Canucks. He was a Phoenix Roadrunner and a Winnipeg Jet in the WHA in 1974–75 and 1976–77. Along the way there were also several minor-league stops, including one in the '80s with the New York Slapshots of the Atlantic Hockey League when he was 48 years old.

Asked recently why he drank so much, he says, "When I was a kid I believed that's what men did — real men. But really, I was scared to death. Scared of myself and the whole world around me. The booze made me feel good. It became more important than the hockey."

It was after Howie was released from a drunk tank in Los Angeles that he called a halt to his boozing. Enough was enough.

Marcel Pronovost, who also successfully fought the bottle, says, "Howie played the tough-guy role but he wasn't a tough kid. He was scared to death of his own blood. If he got a little cut, he would faint."

George Gamester of the *Toronto Star* caught up with Howie recently. He talked to him from his home in tiny Thoreau, New Mexico, where he drives a school bus. "It's been 33 years since I had my last drink," Howie says proudly. "I love these wide open spaces. Got my wife here and a quarter horse named Red and a couple of dogs. If I was any happier I couldn't stand it."

Ex-Wings Shine for '67 Leafs

WHEN the Detroit Red Wings beat the Montreal Canadiens to win the Stanley Cup in April 1955, they assumed the victory parties would keep on coming. But 42 years would pass before another Detroit team would circle the ice as Cup champions. That's a long time to leave the champagne on ice.

In 1967, in an unlikely set of circumstances, no fewer than four of those 1955 Red Wings would play a pivotal role in capturing Lord Stanley's famous mug once again, but with the Toronto Maple Leafs.

Terry Sawchuk, the Wings' Vezina-winning goalie in '55, was joined by defensemen Marcel Pronovost and Larry Hillman, as well as blueliner-turned-center Red Kelly. Under Leaf coach Punch Imlach, the quartet found new life and fresh legs in an upset win over the Montreal Canadiens in the 1967 finals. All four had taken different routes to the Cup win.

Sawchuk had become a Leaf in June 1964 when Sid Abel exposed him in the intra-league draft. Punch Imlach astutely snapped him up. It would be a tandem of 37-year-old Sawchuk and 42-year-old Johnny Bower who led the Leafs to victory over 21-year-old Hab goalie Rogie Vachon.

Red Kelly, who'd enjoyed 13 solid years in Detroit, was traded to the New York Rangers in 1960. But he refused to report and decided to retire. What a furor that caused. NHL President Clarence Campbell indignantly told Kelly, "Young man, you'll never get a job in hockey for as long as you live if you don't get on a plane to New York." Respectful but steadfast, Kelly replied, "If that's the way it has to be, I can live with that, Mr. Campbell. In fact, just today I took a job outside of hockey." King Clancy called the next day, asking if Red would consider playing for the Leafs if it could be arranged. Kelly couldn't resist, and within hours he was a Maple Leaf. In desperation, Jack Adams accepted journeyman defenseman Marc Reaume as compensation for the future Hall of Famer.

Leaf coach Punch Imlach immediately switched Kelly from defense, where'd he'd won the Norris Trophy, to center ice. He excelled as a forward for seven and a half seasons with Toronto, retiring after the 1967 Cup win at age 39. Kelly is the only non–Montreal Canadien to win as many as eight Stanley Cups as a player — four with Detroit and four more with Toronto. Not only was Kelly a hockey star in the mid '60s, he served as a Member of Parliament.

Marcel Pronovost was a fixture on the Red Wings' blueline from 1950 until May 1965, when he was traded to Toronto as part of a blockbuster eight-player deal. By 1967 Pronovost was 36, with more lines in his face than a referee's jersey. Grateful to Imlach for giving him one last shot at a Cup victory, he played extremely well and combined with Larry Hillman on Toronto's most effective defense pair in the playoffs. "Punch was very good to me," Pronovost said recently. "I was making $30,000 in Detroit and he bumped my salary up to $42,000. Then he added an extra $10,000 that season after we won the Cup. It wasn't because I had a bonus clause. He just gave it to me. Heck, in Detroit when we won the Cup, we didn't even get a ring."

Larry Hillman, when he broke in as an 18 year old with Detroit in 1954–55, never dreamed his career would be such a nomadic one, taking him to eight NHL cities and two more in the WHA. Nor could he have imagined that his name would be engraved on the Stanley Cup six times — with Detroit in '55, with Toronto in '62, '63, '64, and '67, and again with Montreal in '69.

His favorite Cup win was with the Leafs in '67 because it was the last year of the six-team league and it's where he feels he contributed the most to his team's success.

The Big M Checks In

SOMEBODY asked the late Punch Imlach once if he was bothered by the public outcry in Toronto following the trade of popular Lanny McDonald to Colorado. "Hell," he said, "people made twice as much fuss over the McDonald trade as they did when I dealt Frank Mahovlich to Detroit. And Mahovlich was twice the player McDonald was."

Imlach and Mahovlich had numerous battles when both were with the Leafs in the '60s. Late in the 1967–68 season, a season in which Mahovlich missed 11 games after he was hospitalized, suffering from nervous tension, Imlach swapped the big left winger to the Red Wings, along with centers Pete Stemkowski and Garry Unger (and the NHL rights to defenseman Carl Brewer) in return for Norm Ullman, Floyd Smith, and Paul Henderson. It was a blockbuster deal.

Mahovlich, then 31, was delighted to be rid of Imlach. In his first full season as a Red Wing, playing with Gordie Howe and Alex Delvecchio, he scored a career high 49 goals. The line set a league record with 118 goals.

Mahovlich recalls driving to Detroit to join his new team after being traded from Toronto. In the car with him were his wife, Marie, and Unger and Stemkowski.

"We went right to the Olympia," he recalls, "and I must say it was located in a very seedy part of town. We looked at our surroundings and nobody said a word. Then Stemkowski broke us up when he sighed, 'Home, sweet home.'"

Mahovlich laughs at another memory. "I was invited to be on a radio call-in show one day and the program zipped right along. The callers were all very friendly and I answered their questions. Then a guy calls in and insults me. He says, 'Hey, Frank, how come you can't skate backwards?"

I bristle and say, 'What do you mean I can't skate backwards?'

"He says, 'I've seen you play. You're lousy at skating backwards.'

"And now I'm getting annoyed. I have my pride. So I challenge the guy. I tell him, 'Listen, pal, you get your skates and come down to the Olympia tomorrow morning. I'll race you backwards around the rink and I guarantee you I'll win.'

"I hear a burst of laughter on the line. Then I recognize the laugh and the voice. It was Pete Stemkowski."

Changes at the Top

Mickey Redmond's Controversial Departure

ICKEY Redmond was just 28 years old on that September day over two decades ago. A new NHL season — 1976–77 — was about to begin and he knew he was not going to be part of it. He picked up the phone and called Red Wings general manager Alex Delvecchio. He told Delvecchio that he couldn't skate, that he was all through, that he'd never play hockey again.

Sure, he was still ticked about a few petty matters, like the time the Wings called a practice on Christmas Day. And he was angry at those who had called him a poor team man and a quitter. But his disagreements with management weren't the reason for his retirement.

The problem was his right leg. Nerve damage had rendered it all but useless. Mickey had tried extensive therapy and rest. He'd seen the team doctor and a number of specialists. But when he skated, when he tried cutting in from the wing, deking and darting to the goalmouth, moves that had once been second nature were now impossible. The power he'd always relied on was gone. His right leg had become dead weight. The knowledge that he was washed up was tough for Mickey to accept. The husky right winger had been the highest-paid Red Wing. Now that paycheck would be gone, and he had a wife and a little girl to support. Another child was on the way. He'd quit school in Grade 12 to pursue his dream of becoming an NHLer, and so he had few marketable skills.

Mind you, he'd fulfilled most of his dreams. Four years with the Montreal Canadiens. Then a trade to Detroit midway through the 1970–71 season — for Frank Mahovlich, no less (along with Bill Collins and Guy Charron). In 1972 he earned a coveted spot on Team Canada's roster, and shared in the glory of that unforgettable victory over the Soviets.

Redmond blossomed in Detroit, scoring 42 goals in his first full season as a Red Wing and 52 the next. No Red Wing — not even Gordie Howe, Norm Ullman, or Frank Mahovlich — had ever before achieved the 50-goal plateau. His scoring prowess brought Redmond a whopping big raise and he showed his appreciation with a 51-goal season in 1973–74.

Mickey could pinpoint when his downfall began. Just as the 1974–75 season was getting under way, he'd begun suffering from back pain. As most hockey players with a nagging injury do, he tried to play through it. But when the pain became so intense he couldn't bend over to lace up his skates, Redmond went to see a specialist. The diagnosis: a ruptured disk.

He was placed in traction and was hospitalized for almost a month. When the pain subsided, he rejoined the Wings. But further tests showed a ruptured disk was pressing on a nerve. On December 20, surgeons wheeled Redmond into the operating room.

The doctors called the operation a success and gave Mickey permission to return to hockey in March. By then, the back pain was gone, but his right leg still wasn't functioning properly.

He finished the season and tested the leg in training camp the following September. He couldn't skate, couldn't score, but he refused to quit. He struggled through each game until a January 18 clash with Los Angeles. After that game he told Delvecchio, "That's it. I need some sick leave."

He flew to Toronto, where he was examined by Dr. Charles Bull, a prominent medical man who had earned Mickey's respect during the Team Canada–Soviet series in 1972. Dr. Bull confirmed that there had been severe damage to the nerve controlling messages from Redmond's brain to his right leg. And additional pressure was being placed on the nerve from a disk adjoining the one that had been removed. Dr. Bull predicted that Redmond would never be completely cured.

The Red Wings, meanwhile, arranged for Mickey to visit the

renowned Mayo Clinic in Rochester, Minnesota. He was admitted and was told that extensive nerve damage in the right leg had been found. One of the specialists there urged him to retire from hockey.

Before he could make a decision about his future, a message from Red Wings management jolted him. GM Alex Delvecchio had suspended Redmond and placed him on waivers. "Look," Delvecchio told newsmen, "he's missed 10 games. We've gone long enough without him. He doesn't want to play in Detroit, otherwise he'd be here."

NHL president Clarence Campbell was as surprised as Redmond at the announcement. After checking the medical evidence, and possibly fearing legal action, Campbell ordered the Wings to reinstate the crippled winger.

Delvecchio refused to believe Redmond's condition was as bad as reported, especially when he learned his injured star had been seen playing tennis. "If he can play tennis, he can play hockey," an angry Delvecchio stated. "His back is killing him, his leg is shot. And yet he can play tennis. Seems to me Mickey Redmond is no team man. If he was, he'd be playing for us right now. Not once did he even come around to the arena."

Dr. Bull came to Redmond's defense. "You can't compare a game of tennis with hockey," he said. "A mild game of tennis isn't going to hurt him."

Redmond admitted he had played tennis, lobbing the ball back and forth with a pal, but that he had not played energetically, and certainly hadn't put much stress on his leg.

Alan Eagleson, Redmond's agent at the time, told sports journalist Earl McRae, "Mickey is no quitter. To suggest he'd rather take the money and run because he doesn't want to play with some pain is an insult to his intelligence and his heart."

Delvecchio countered, "He gave us the impression things were fine, that he'd be back. He really screwed us up."

Throughout the spring and summer of 1976, Redmond embarked on a fitness program. With training camp approaching, he tested his leg again, hoping for some sign of recovery. The limb failed the test. He knew at that moment his playing career was over.

In those days, I was a color commentator with *Hockey Night in Canada*. One night host Dave Hodge and I heard Mickey Redmond on a Red Wing radio broadcast. We were both impressed and recommended him to Ralph Mellanby, our executive producer. Before long, Mickey joined us as a regular commentator on *Hockey Night in Canada*. Broadcasting seemed to come naturally to him. Eventually he would return to Detroit, where for the past dozen years, he has been a color commentator on the Red Wings' telecasts.

Habs Blame Wings for Playoff Miss

CAN you believe the Red Wings almost caused a team to start a game without a goaltender?

It happened late in the 1969–70 NHL season during a wild battle for playoff positions between the Canadiens, Bruins, Red Wings, Blackhawks, and Rangers. When the season ended, the East Division standings looked like this:

Team	G	W	L	T	GF	GA	PTS
Chicago	76	45	22	9	250	170	99
Boston	76	40	17	19	277	216	99
Detroit	76	40	21	15	246	199	95
New York	76	38	22	16	246	189	92
Montreal	76	38	22	16	244	201	92
Toronto	76	29	34	13	222	242	71

The difference between first and fifth place was a mere seven points. It was the closest playoff race in NHL history and it all came down to the final weekend. On the final Sunday of the season, the fifth-place Rangers were two points behind the Canadiens. A New York win combined with a Montreal loss would leave the teams tied. Both teams would also have identical records, 38–22–16, so the coveted playoff spot would then go to whichever team had scored the most goals.

The Rangers were slated to host the Red Wings in a nationally televised matinee from Madison Square Garden. For the Wings, there was nothing at stake: they were in third place no matter what. New York scored three times on Roger Crozier in the first 13 minutes. By the end of the game, New York had scored nine times.

In Chicago to play the Blackhawks that night, the Canadiens' players were furious, accusing the Wings of lying down, of not even trying. No one accused Detroit of actually throwing the game, but their lack of effort was called inexcusable.

The Habs were further incensed when Red Wing star Garry Unger was interviewed during the intermission and candidly admitted that his team had been out partying the night before.

The New York win meant Montreal needed a tie or a win against the Hawks to make the playoffs. And there was no chance Chicago would stand aside the way Detroit appeared to have done, because Chicago badly needed a win to keep their hold on first place.

As a result of Detroit's ineptitude, the Canadiens faced a dilemma. Rather than play for a win or tie, Habs coach Claude Ruel and GM Sam Pollock actually considered starting the game without a goaltender. The idea was to use six attackers and score at least five goals as quickly as possible to surpass the Rangers' total. There was no rule against this bizarre plan, but it certainly would have harmed the integrity of the game.

After much debate the Habs opted to play it straight. In the third period they found themselves trailing 3–2 — one goal more (a tie) would put them in the playoffs. Suddenly, Chicago's Pit Martin raced in twice and scored both times. Now there was 9:16 left to play and the Hawks were up 5–2. With their hopes of a win or tie dashed, the Canadiens went to plan B.

Coach Claude Ruel pulled Rogie Vachon from the net in favor of a sixth attacker. No team in history had ever pulled its goalie with so much time left to play, but Montreal hoped to score the three goals they now needed to top the Rangers. Seconds later, Chicago's Eric Nesterenko slipped the puck into the open cage. Then Cliff Koroll scored. His goal was followed by a Bobby Hull blast. Then Bobby's brother Dennis ripped one into the Montreal net. With three seconds left, Gerry Pinder wrapped up the Chicago scoring spree. Final score: Chicago 10, Montreal 2.

The Canadiens had missed the playoffs for the first time in 22 years. And they placed most of the blame on the Detroit Red Wings. "I say that Detroit coach Sid Abel and his players were the real culprits for not putting out against New York," John Ferguson said bitterly.

A Coaching Oddity

CAN an NHL coach be charged with a loss in a game he had nothing to do with? It happened to Alex Delvecchio during the 1973–74 season.

On November 7, 1973, the Red Wings decided to release coach Ted Garvin — 2–8–1 after 11 games — and replace him with Alex Delvecchio. But Delvecchio had not yet retired as a player, and since NHL rules barred playing coaches, Garvin was asked to stay on for the game that night. Garvin reluctantly agreed but, with just under three minutes to play and the Wings headed for another defeat, he left the rink in disgust. Forward Tim Ecclestone, not dressed for the game that night, stepped in and handled the line changes for the remainder of the contest. Strangely, but officially, the loss that night went on Delvecchio's coaching record, even though he neither played in the contest nor stood behind the bench.

Polonich Clubbed
by Paiement

ON August 17, 1982, the first civil lawsuit resulting from an on-ice incident in the NHL ended with former Red Wing Dennis Polonich receiving an award of $850,000 from a U.S. Federal Court.

The incident that triggered the lawsuit took place during a game between Detroit and Colorado on October 25, 1978, at the Olympia. Polonich was struck in the face by a stick wielded by the Rockies' Wilf Paiement. The blow broke Polonich's nose and inflicted other facial injuries. Dr. John Finley, the Red Wing physician who treated Polonich, called it "the worst injury he'd ever seen." Detroit general manager Ted Lindsay testified that Paiement hit Polonich in the manner of a baseball player swinging a bat.

As a result of the attack, the NHL suspended Paiement for 15 games and fined him $500. The lawsuit followed with Polonich arguing his injuries had shortened his career. Attempts to settle the dispute out of court proved fruitless.

The amount of the award stunned the hockey world, especially when Polonich's attorney, James Feeney, revealed that he had been prepared to settle for less than $100,000. Paiement's attorney called the amount of the award "totally unreasonable."

At a golf tournament in British Columbia in the summer of 1997 I talked with Polonich. "I was surprised that Paiement never showed any remorse for clubbing me," he said. "As for the damages, none of the money came out of his pocket. He was insured.

"My career went downhill after the injury and I had hopes that the Red Wings might offer me something in the way of a coaching or management opportunity. I was disappointed when it didn't happen." Polonich has been a successful coach in junior hockey for the past dozen years, in places like Yorkton, Saskatchewan; Medicine Hat, Alberta; and Prince George, British Columbia.

When I asked Dennis if the settlement figure I'd read about so many years ago was an accurate one, or if he received an amount far less than the $850,000, he laughed and said, "Oh, I got the full amount and then some. With interest, you know, and smart investments it worked out very well for me, well over a million."

Proud To Be a Red Wing

IS Dennis Polonich proud to be a former Red Wing?

"Sure I am," he says. "Nobody expected me to make the team, to become an NHLer. I was an 8th round draft choice, after all — and small; I was only five foot five and 160 pounds. And I was a center when the team had Alex Delvecchio, Red Berenson, and Marcel Dionne at the position. Try to beat one of those guys out of a job.

"Let me tell you a funny story about Dionne. The Wings were playing an exhibition game one night against St. Louis, and Marcel got sick and couldn't play. So I was called in at the last minute and there was no time to get an extra jersey for me. The trainer gave me Dionne's number 5. This was before they put the names on the backs of the jerseys. So a lot of the fans thought I was Marcel. We're both short and stocky, see.

"Now, a big fight breaks out and I get excited. I leap over the boards and grab one of the St. Louis Blues and boom! I knocked the guy flat. One punch. The crowd goes wild. They're screaming, 'Marcel! Marcel!' Now, Marcel couldn't fight. He never got into fights. But on this night the fans thought he was a slugger, one of the best damn fighters they'd ever seen.

"Another thing I'm proud of," he says, "is the fact I played against Gordie Howe and his sons in the last game he played at the Olympia. My line started against Gordie and the boys. And at the end of the game, I went right over and asked Gordie for his stick. So I have the last stick he used at the Olympia. After he gave me the stick, he took a lap around the ice and the crowd went crazy. They loved the guy. And he took off a glove and threw it high in the stands. Then he skated across the ice and threw his other glove. I've never heard such an ovation."

Little-Known Facts About Gordie Howe

YOU'VE read everything written about Detroit's greatest player, seen and heard all the interviews on TV and radio. You figure you know all about the guy.

How many of the following facts are you familiar with?

- It's been written that Gordie played his first hockey in Floral, Saskatchewan. If he did he was the youngest player on the team because the Howe family moved from Floral to Saskatoon a mere five days after Gordie's birth.
- When the fans honored Gordie one night in 1959, Detroit management surprised him by flying his parents in from Saskatoon. It was Gordie's 13th NHL season, yet it was the first time they'd seen him play — except on TV.
- Surely you've heard the story about Gordie's first pair of skates. A poor lady came to the Howe household in Saskatoon and exchanged a sack full of items for some milk money. When a pair of skates fell out of the sack, Gordie grabbed one and his sister Edna pounced on the

other. Together they glided across the ice in the backyard — each using one skate. When Edna left her skate lying around one day, Gordie grabbed it and she never got it back. Later, Gordie's dad took his old street shoes and affixed metal blades to them. They were homemade skates, but they worked.

- A mischievous youngster, Gordie was at the rink in Saskatoon one night when a fight broke out during a pro game. When all eyes were on the scuffle on the ice, young Howe raced over and stole an armful of hockey sticks from one of the teams. Later, he distributed the sticks to his friends, keeping a good one for himself.

- Gordie began his career in minor hockey as a goaltender. He could play any position well and was a member of as many as five teams in a season.

- At age 16, Gordie attended a Detroit training camp and signed a contract. He was assigned to the Wings' junior team in Galt, but sat out the entire season because of an administrative problem. At the time, the Red Wings considered a player named Terry Cavanaugh to be the better prospect. Cavanaugh never played a game in the NHL, but he did become mayor of Edmonton.

- Gordie turned pro in 1945 at age 17. He was sent to Omaha and was paid $2,350 for the season. He was promised a Red Wings jacket as a bonus but didn't receive it until two years later — after he reminded Jack Adams he hadn't kept his word.

- Howe enjoyed catching unwary bystanders with his "snow on the stick" routine. He'd load up the blade of his stick with snow and slush and victimize cameramen and TV commentators in the middle of an interview at rinkside, dousing them with a faceful of slush. He was particularly adept at this in the days when chicken wire rather than Plexiglas surrounded the ends of rinks. It was a favorite way to silence mouthy fans.

- Gordie figures he's had about 500 stitches in his face and he's had his nose broken 14 times.

- Gordie brought son Mark, then a toddler, into the Red

Wings dressing room one day when Jack Adams stormed in and began lecturing the players in a loud, profane manner. During a break in the tirade, Mark piped up, "Hey, Dad, who's that fat old guy?"

- In 1979 Gordie became the first and only grandfather to score a goal in the NHL. He potted one against Edmonton on his first shift to celebrate the birth of his son Mark's firstborn, Travis Howe.
- In a game against Montreal, Rocket Richard sped down the ice on a breakaway. Howe jumped over the boards onto the ice and checked him, drawing a two-minute penalty for too many men on the ice.
- Gordie was set to play a game in 1990 for the Los Angeles Kings, alongside Wayne Gretzky. That would have made him the only NHLer to perform in six decades. But the Hartford Whalers, who owned his rights, said, "No way. If the old guy plays for anybody, he plays for us." Gordie would eventually play one shift in the '90s, but with the Detroit Vipers of the International Hockey League.
- Former Leaf captain Sid Smith says, "I ran Gordie into the boards one night and he turned, grabbed me by the throat with one hand, and lifted me right off the ice. When I got back to the bench, coach Hap Day said, 'Why didn't you belt the guy?' I said, 'I would have, but he wouldn't put me down.'"

Abel Forced Out

WHEN Sid Abel, who served the Red Wings for more than 30 years as a player, captain, coach, and executive, resigned as general manager on January 6, 1971, he lashed out at two newcomers to the Detroit organization, Jim Bishop and Ned Harkness.

Asked to assess the coaching talents of Harkness, who'd compiled a record of 163–27–2 at Cornell University, Abel bluntly replied, "I can't because I don't think he is a coach. In fact, he is not a coach. I don't think he can change lines or do other things a coach must be able to do to stay in the NHL. He sure can talk, though. I didn't believe it was possible for a guy to come in — I didn't hire him — and in four months force me to step aside.

"All of our problems started a year earlier when Mr. Bishop came on the scene [as the Red Wings' executive director]. I'm sure Mr. Norris is more aware now that he was sold a bill of goods by Mr. Bishop and Mr. Harkness. I don't like to say I was squeezed out by those two so I'll say I am going out on my own."

Bishop had arrived in Detroit with a pro lacrosse franchise, which he sold to Bruce Norris, and stayed on with the Red Wings as an executive when the sport died in the city. He recommended Harkness, another lacrosse enthusiast, for the Red Wings' coaching job then held by Abel.

Informed of Abel's bitter remarks, Harkness said, "I'm sorry Mr. Abel has made the comments he did. They demean me personally and professionally and I don't think anyone benefits by remarks of this nature. I am more than willing to stand on my record as a coach."

Harkness's record as a college coach was far superior to the results he got in his abbreviated stint with the Wings. In 38 games, his Red Wings won 12 games, lost 22, and tied 4. In January 1971, he was promoted to the general manager's job in Detroit. During Harkness's four years as either coach or GM, the Wings came in seventh, fifth, fifth, and sixth in the East Division.

Colleen Howe Helps Engineer a Coup

NO hockey wife has been closer to the scene than Colleen Howe. With a husband and two sons in pro hockey, she has taken a keen interest in the game and some of the bizarre people in it. She has been a shrewd negotiator, fiercely protective of the men in her family. Her hockey career has been almost as interesting as Gordie's.

For example, Colleen discovered that the World Hockey Association had no restrictions against signing underage draft choices when the league made its debut in 1972. Like everybody else, she assumed the new league could not draft junior players until they'd reached the age of 20. But her secretary, Dorothy Ringler, was told during some discreet inquires to league president Gary Davidson that there was no league bylaw prohibiting teenagers from playing in the WHA. What amazed Colleen was that Davidson had not distributed this information to the member clubs of the WHA and that Davidson himself hadn't been aware that there wasn't a bylaw until asked to look it up.

This loophole was exciting news to Colleen, who just happened to have under her own roof two of the brightest young prospects in the game — Mark and Marty Howe. Both were coming off a Memorial Cup–winning season with the Toronto Marlboros.

While her sons and Gordie were celebrating the Memorial Cup victory in the dressing room, Colleen talked with Bill Dineen and Doug Harvey, two old friends who were organizing the new WHA team in Houston. Both men, unaware of the loophole, thought it was a shame that the Howe boys could not be drafted. Colleen suggested that Dineen and Harvey contact Gary Davidson for clarification of the underage draft rules. Perhaps her two sons would be eligible for the WHA draft after all.

Dineen verified with Davidson that the Howes and any other teenagers were eligible for the draft. Incredibly, Davidson didn't notify the other WHA teams about this important ruling, one that would eventually change the face of modern hockey.

On draft day, Dineen stunned his WHA rivals by drafting both Mark and Marty. The other WHA teams, caught napping, were furious. They accused Dineen of breaking the rules and wasting his picks. But Davidson made it clear that the WHA had no rules protecting teenagers from the draft — only the NHL did that.

Later that day, Bobby Hull, at that time with the Winnipeg Jets, made a prediction. "Just wait," he said. "With the Howe boys in Houston, it won't be long before they talk to Gordie and coax him out of retirement. The Jets should draft Gordie and then we at least can trade with Houston and get a good player for him." But Hull's associates thought it was a crazy idea. Gordie, they said, was too old to make a comeback. It'll never happen.

The WHA's drafting of the Howe boys upset the NHL moguls terribly. NHL President Clarence Campbell called Gordie and Colleen and tried to convince them that a move to the new league by her sons would be the ruination of junior hockey. So Colleen offered Campbell an alternative. She suggested that the NHL match the salaries offered by the Houston club, put the money into a trust fund, and make it available to her sons when they became eligible for NHL play. Mr. Campbell took the proposal to the NHL Board of Governors, who turned it down flat. It was a costly decision. Other junior stars, now able to command huge salaries, followed the Howes' lead, and gave the upstart league exciting new talent and credibility.

And it wasn't long before the Aeros proved Bobby Hull right and convinced Gordie, at age 45, to suit up. Howe won the MVP award in his first season in the WHA. In four seasons as a Houston Aero, he scored 100, 99, 102, and 68 points (he missed 16 games in his final season because of injury), respectively.

Kromm's Success Didn't Last

IN 1977 coach Bobby Kromm arrived in Detroit with some impressive credentials. He'd won a world championship for Canada as coach of the amateur Trail Smoke Eaters and he'd won an Avco Cup as coach of the Winnipeg Jets in the World Hockey Association. In the Chicago Blackhawks' farm system he'd won three Central Hockey League championships in places like St. Louis and Dallas and was named coach of the year with the latter club.

With that kind of success, it's no wonder Detroit signed him as coach in 1977, especially after the Wings had set a team futility record for fewest wins (16) the previous season.

Under the Calgary-born Kromm, there was a remarkable improvement. The Wings earned 37 more points in 1977–78, posting a 32–34–14 record, good enough for 78 points and second place in their division behind Montreal. It was the only year during a 13-season stretch from 1970–71 through 1982–83 that the Wings made the playoffs. They went on to win their first-round playoff series with the Atlanta Flames before the Canadiens of Lafleur, Shutt, Robinson, Lemaire, and Gainey, winners of 59 games during the regular season, eliminated them in five games in round two.

Somehow, Kromm seemed able to get the most out of his players that year. Detroit fans anticipated further improvement in '78–'79. But it was not to be. In the off-season, management acquired goaltender Rogie Vachon from the Los Angeles Kings, but Vachon's best days were behind him. Several other players Kromm had been counting on played poorly. The team skidded all the way into last place in the Norris Division with a dismal 23–41–16 record for 62 points. Only two other clubs in the league fared worse.

Late in the 1979–80 season, with Detroit engaged with four other clubs in a life-and-death struggle for the last two spots in the 16-team playoff tournament, general manager Ted Lindsay fired Kromm and took the coaching job himself. The Wings were 24–36–11 when Kromm was dismissed. His overall record as coach was 79–111–41.

Under Lindsay, the Wings weren't exactly galvanized. They won but two of their last nine games and missed the playoffs by six points. The highlight of the season wasn't even a Red Wing moment. It took place in a March 12 game against Hartford when, for the first time in history, a father-and-son combination played in the NHL. Gordie Howe played on a line with his sons Mark and Marty at the Olympia, and the cheering was the loudest heard all season.

Dionne Slips Away

AFTER four seasons as a Red Wing, including a 1974–75 season in which he'd jumped from 78 to 121 points, Marcel Dionne stunned the Wings by spurning the richest contract ever offered a Detroit player and announcing he wanted to play elsewhere.

It was reported that Dionne wanted out of Detroit because of the city's high crime rate. He'd been upset when teammate Guy Charron was held up in the parking lot outside the Olympia after a practice.

The Wings did everything they could to keep Dionne. He was offered a $1-million package to stay. Coach Alex Delvecchio made him the team captain and brought Sid Abel's number 12 out of retirement to give to the young centerman who'd finished third in league scoring in 1974–75. Dionne's 47 goals established a club record for a Detroit center and his 121 points were the most in Red Wing history. His brilliant playmaking resulted in a 50-goal season for linemate Danny Grant.

However, Dionne walked out on the Wings a couple of times and was suspended. He was described as a malcontent, and on one occasion attacked a sportswriter. He played out his option and became a free agent. Later, he told a reporter, "It's so difficult playing in Detroit. The owner put a lot of pressure on everyone. Managers, coaches, and players were always coming and going. Perhaps I've behaved like a little boy at times, speaking out of turn and acting hastily. But I think I'm growing up."

The Toronto Maple Leafs made a strong pitch for Dionne, but they couldn't or wouldn't match the offer made by Los Angeles Kings owner Jack Kent Cooke. Cooke traded two veterans — Dan Maloney and Terry Harper — and threw in journeyman Bart Crashley for Dionne, then made him the second-highest paid player in the league by signing him to a five-year, $1.5 million contract.

When Stu Nahan, a sportscaster in Los Angeles, called the deal a coup, Cooke corrected him. "It was much more than a coup," he said. "It was a steal."

The 50th Anniversary

THE game at the Olympia on the night of November 24, 1976, was special not only because of the 4–3 win over the Toronto Maple Leafs — it also marked the 50th anniversary of the storied franchise.

Prior to the game, Budd Lynch — for 25 years the voice of Red Wing hockey — served as the master of ceremonies. Standing under the spotlights at center ice, Lynch introduced the evening's special guests.

First, three new members were inducted into the Red Wings Hall of Fame: Tommy Ivan, coach of the Wings for seven years; Jimmy Skinner, a former coach and currently the assistant general manager; and Marguerite Norris Riker, team president in the 1950s and the first woman to have her name engraved on the Stanley Cup.

Then the spotlight played over the stands, picking out people associated with those great days. First was Mrs. Helen Adams, wife of the late "Mr. Hockey," Jack Adams. Then there was Mrs. Nick Londes, widow of former Olympia general manager Nick Londes. The spotlight's beam fell upon a hundred more members of the Red Wings alumni, many of them Hall of Famers.

Next, Lynch directed the crowd's attention to the entrance-way to the ice — for the reuniting of the famed Production Line. First came Ted Lindsay, a very successful businessman in partnership with former teammate Marty Pavelich, and at the time very active in hockey with the Red Wing alumni and as coach of Hillsdale College. Then came Sid "Boot" Abel, a premier centerman in his day, later coach and general manager of the Red Wings, then general manager of the Kansas City Scouts, and back with Detroit in the broadcast booth.

Then there was a deafening roar of applause, and everyone in the arena was on their feet to honor old Number Nine, Gordie Howe. The greatest hockey player in the world was back on Olympia ice, and it was as if he'd never left.

Among the players lined up along the blue lines, center Dennis Polonich couldn't keep his eyes off the Red Wing legend. "I want to meet Gordie," he told Terry Harper. "I can't wait to see him after the game. You know, shake his hand . . ."

"Why wait?" Harper laughed. "Go over now."

Without pausing, Polonich dashed over to where Gordie was standing and grabbed him by the hand. The crowd roared. The other players followed suit and a long line formed behind Polonich.

Wrong Man, Wrong Time, Wrong Place

REMEMBER Ned Harkness? He was coach and later general manager of the Detroit Red Wings for a few seasons in the '70s. He'd built up a big reputation in U.S. college hockey with RPI and Cornell, then became the first man to jump from campus rinks to coach in the pros, only to fall flat on his back in the Motor City.

What happened? Was it Ned's rah-rah approach, treating the pros like college kids, that killed his chances in Detroit? Or was Fred Shero right when he said, "Harkness had many things going for him but hockey players and club owners are afraid of outsiders"?

There's no question Harkness jolted the Wings right from day one. At training camp he introduced new methods — including a novel forechecking system and some interesting conditioning drills. His chalk talks annoyed the veterans, who complained about being treated like "collegians." Gordie Howe, Alex Delvecchio, and Frank Mahovlich all got their digs in.

Harkness fought back, pointing the finger at general manager Sid Abel. He complained about the complacency within the organization. He griped about the lack of scouting reports and he was annoyed when Abel told him, "Don't worry, Ned. Things will work out."

Eventually Abel, irritated by the criticism, delivered an ultimatum to team owner Bruce Norris. "Either Harkness goes or I go."

Norris replied, "We're going to miss you, Sid. I'm sticking with Harkness."

But the veteran players sided with Abel. Like them, he was from the old school. The Red Wings drew up a petition stating that if Harkness wasn't fired, they would refuse to play. Gordie Howe was chosen to deliver the edict to Bruce Norris. Still the owner backed Harkness, and asked him to be both coach *and* general manager. But Harkness knew by now that the Wings were never going to play his style of hockey. He resigned as coach and assumed Abel's old job as general manager.

The venomous stories spread about Harkness by the players and relayed in the press earned him the fans' contempt. His car windows were broken and his home was splattered with eggs. One fan attacked him physically, while others sent death threats and hate mail by the bagful to the Red Wing offices.

By February 1974, the situation had become intolerable. Harkness resigned from the organization, offering no explanation, except to say, "I guess I was the wrong man, with the wrong team, at the wrong time."

I knew Ned Harkness long before he reached the NHL. Our St. Lawrence University hockey teams often played against his RPI squads in the '50s. Harkness was the greatest college hockey coach I'd ever seen. He was known as the Miracle Man of RPI for his ability to take teams with little depth right to the heights. In 1954, his RPI team had two lines, a pair of defensemen, and a goalie. He guided it past powerhouses Michigan and Minnesota to win the NCAA title. His record at RPI was 187–90–7, despite the fact his teams were always thin on talent.

In the '60s he moved on to Cornell and molded a hockey powerhouse. And that was in his first three years on the job, before he'd had a chance to stock his team with players he'd recruited personally. From 1967 to 1970 Cornell captured two national titles, four straight East Coast Athletic Conference crowns, and five straight Ivy League championships. One of his stars was goalie Ken Dryden, who played in only three losing games during his college career. During one stretch in 1970, Cornell went a record 29 games without a loss.

After the disaster in Detroit, Harkness embarked on a program to bring top college hockey to Union College in Schenectady, New York. He began with no arena and no team and, putting together a team of freshmen and sophomores, he quickly ran up a record of 48–6–2 against varsity competition. He resigned in 1978, blaming interference from college administrators. "I'm a hockey coach, not a politician," Harkness said.

Not Your Normal Pre-Game Meal

THE late George Hayes, one of hockey's most colorful and eccentric linesmen, liked to save a little money on road trips by packing his own lunches. One day he packed some canned meat and some fresh bread in his bag, added a "pop" or two to wash things down, and jumped on the train for Detroit. He opened the canned meat, spread the contents on the bread, added thick chunks of onion on top, and sat back to enjoy his meal. It was only when he went to throw the empty can in the trash that he noticed a photo of a dog on the label.

"I admit I'd had a snort or two beforehand," he told referee Red Storey, when the two friends met before a game in Detroit. "But I can't believe I made sandwiches out of dog food. Whatever you do, Red, don't breathe a word of this to anybody."

Red gave his word, but he was never one to keep quiet, especially not when a good laugh was assured. As the players took the ice for their pre-game warm-up, some of the Red Wings skated close to Hayes.

"Arf, arf!" they barked. "Ruff, ruff."

"They kept barkin' at me all game," said Hayes. "Some of them even called me 'Pard' [a brand of dog food]. I was ready to kill that big-mouth Storey."

7

Ilitch Takes Charge

Breaking All the Rules

URING the 1988–89 season coach Jacques Demers and Red Wings' management had more dealings with police officers, customs officials, rehab centers, and lawyers than they did with players and agents.

A look through the pages of *The Hockey News* that season reveals the following:

September 23: Peter Klima and Bob Probert were suspended by the Red Wings for a series of infractions, including missed curfews, practices, and scheduled team flights.

October 9: Peter Klima, a previous offender for drunken driving, faced the strong possibility of a jail sentence after a second arrest on the same charge. He was charged with leaving the scene of an accident and improperly backing up a vehicle, striking another vehicle.

November 23: Kim Cavanaugh, a 23-year-old Boston woman, filed charges with police, accusing Detroit right winger Joey Kocur of assault and battery. She alleged her nose was broken while she was driving Kocur back to his hotel. A similar charge had been brought against Kocur by a 21-year-old Detroit woman, Janet Maschke, after an August 23 incident in which she alleged Kocur slugged her in the arm outside a bar.

January 25: Bob Probert, 23, was suspended and sent home when he showed up 25 minutes late for a game with Buffalo. He told club officials he was delayed in traffic. "Management told him to stay away from the team?" one of Probert's teammates asked in mock surprise. "Hey, he's been doing a pretty good job of that all on his own."

March 2: A packet containing 14.2 grams of cocaine fell out of Bob Probert's underwear during an early-morning strip search by U.S. customs agents on the American side of the Detroit–Windsor tunnel. Probert was arraigned on a single count of smuggling narcotics into the U.S. If convicted, he would face up to 20 years in prison and a fine of up to $1 million.

March 4: NHL president John Ziegler expelled Bob Probert from the league, and the Red Wings announced they were writing him off the payroll.

Probert was the fifth player banned from the NHL for drug offenses. The others were: Don Murdoch of the New York Rangers, in 1978–79; Ric Nattress of Montreal, in 1983; Toronto's Borje Salming in 1986–87; and Edmonton goalie Grant Fuhr, in 1990–91. Murdoch's punishment for possessing 4.8 grams of cocaine was a one-year suspension, later reduced to 40 games. Nattress had been handed a one-year suspension, later reduced to 30 games, for possession of marijuana and hashish; Salming served an eight-game suspension (plus four preseason games) after he admitted he'd experimented with cocaine several years earlier; and Fuhr received a one-year suspension, later reduced to 60 games.

March 21: A federal grand jury returned an indictment formalizing charges against Bob Probert. It was noted that, prior to the March 2 incident, Probert had been banned from entering the country because of three previous arrests on charges of driving while intoxicated. A waiver on the ban was granted when Probert's lawyer indicated that his client was seeking professional help.

May 1989: Petr Klima was arrested for drunk driving — his third such arrest in two years. He was also charged with resisting arrest and driving with a suspended license.

Also in May, federal prosecutors asked a judge to jail Bob Probert pending his trial on cocaine-smuggling charges. Interim U.S. Attorney Stephen Markham told the court Probert had twice left a substance abuse center without authorization — once with the help of another patient's wife, the other time with the aid of a nurse. The judge revoked Probert's driver's license and suspended his telephone privileges and visitation rights.

June 1989: Red Wing forward Petr Klima was sentenced to 35 days in jail after his May drunk-driving charge and was ordered to enter a substance-abuse center for 45 days upon his release.

Meanwhile, forward Joey Kocur, who'd pleaded guilty to disorderly conduct in the Janet Maschke assault case, was awaiting trial in Boston for the charges brought in November 1988 by Kim Cavanaugh. Kocur and Cavanaugh also filed civil charges against each other, seeking damages.

June 11: Bob Probert's lawyer, Patrick Ducharme of Windsor, Ontario, was charged with driving while under the influence of alcohol. He was also charged with refusing to take a preliminary blood alcohol test.

July 18: Bob Probert appeared before judge Patrick Duggan and pleaded guilty to importing cocaine. Sentencing was set for September 26, 1989.

Late July 1989: Red Wing insiders said owner Mike Ilitch snapped when he heard that Steve Chiasson, leading scorer among Detroit defensemen, had been arrested for drunk driving. Ilitch promised swifter and more decisive measures against Red Wing players caught abusing drugs and alcohol.

October 17: Bob Probert was sentenced to three months in prison, put on three years' probation, and fined $2,000 for smuggling cocaine into the United States.

October 26: Bob Probert was told he would have to wait until December before learning whether he would be deported as a result of his felony drug conviction.

October 31: A Hamilton, Ontario, man was charged with offering a bribe, obstruction of justice, and conspiracy over an alleged scheme to fix Bob Probert's cocaine-smuggling case. The man, Dan Defrancesco, was charged with trying to bribe an undercover agent who'd been posing as a U.S. customs official. The agent was allegedly asked to lose the evidence against Probert.

November 1989: NHL president John Ziegler met with Bob Probert and came away satisfied that he was committed to rehabilitation. Mr. Ziegler hinted that Probert could be back in hockey as early as March 5, 1990. "Mr. Probert has paid a very severe price," Ziegler said. "He will have lost in excess of $200,000 in salary and will have to expend up to $90,000 in legal fees. Not to mention the nearly eight months he has spent in a rehabilitation center north of Detroit and the three-month term he spent in a Minnesota prison."

January 1990: A Chicago immigration judge ordered Bob Probert deported to Canada. Marshal Hyman, a member of Probert's legal team, said the decision would be appealed. Probert, meanwhile, played on a prison hockey team. After a game, the winners had received a six-pack of soft drinks.

March 1990: A week of good news for Bob Probert. On March 5, he began skating by himself at Joe Louis Arena. On March 7, the U.S. Immigration and Naturalization Service issued him a 90-day work permit, and, on March 9, NHL president John Ziegler reinstated the Detroit right winger. When informed of Probert's possible return to the Wings, his former teammates were enthused. "If and when he returns, he'll be welcomed warmly," Steve Yzerman said. "You can't keep kicking a guy and knocking him down. He's done his time. He's proven he wants to come back. And we're in full support."

March 22, 1990: Probation officers and the Red Wings decided to allow Probert to play in a March 22 game versus Minnesota. The Wings were crushed 5–1. When Probert hopped over the boards for his first shift in a year and 21 days, the crowd welcomed him with a prolonged ovation. He scored a goal in each of his first three games back, including the lone goal in the loss to Minnesota, the game-winner in a 5–3 victory over Chicago two days later, and a tying goal in a 3–2 loss to Chicago March 25. He also won three fights and logged 21 penalty minutes.

"He's an amazing athlete to do what he did," coach Jacques Demers said. "I've never seen anything like it."

May 9: Bob Probert made the first of several visits to schools in the Detroit area, urging students to stay away from drugs. He said he expected to return to the Wings, but not on a full-time basis, since he was not allowed to cross the border into Canada.

In July 1994, Probert left the Red Wings as a free agent and signed a contract with the Chicago Blackhawks. His best season in Detroit was in 1987–88 when he scored 29 goals and added 33 assists for 62 points. He also led the league in penalty minutes with 398 minutes.

Trade to Detroit Leaves Sittler Bitter

T HE last few years of Darryl Sittler's NHL career, including his final season, as a Red Wing, were miserable ones. His troubles began in the late '70s when he captained the Maple Leafs. Despite scoring between 80 and 100 points each season, and setting a league record with 10 points in one game in 1976, he found himself constantly at loggerheads with team owner Harold Ballard and general manager Punch Imlach. At one point Ballard treated Sittler "like he was my son," but a few months later was calling him a "cancer on my hockey team."

Finally, during the 1981–82 season, Sittler waived a no-trade clause in his contract and allowed himself to be dealt to Philadelphia, where he thrived on the change of scene. He enjoyed playing with great stars like Bobby Clarke, Tim Kerr, and Bill Barber, and he clicked for 43 goals and 83 points in his first full season as a Flyer. The following season, playing less because management had decided to give veterans more rest, Sittler collected 27 goals.

In the summer of 1984, Bobby Clarke retired as a player to take over as the Flyers' new general manager, and he promptly hired Mike Keenan as the team's new coach. Sittler had been told he would be introduced as Philadelphia's new team captain — replacing Clarke — at the end of training camp. He was even advised to prepare an acceptance speech, because the announcement would be made at the annual meet-the-team luncheon.

Prior to the luncheon, the media interviewed Darryl about his new duties as team captain, but strangely, when Clarke got up to speak, he failed to announce that Sittler was his choice as captain. Sittler, and the reporters he'd been talking to, were confused. Later that afternoon, Bobby Clarke called Sittler into his office and stunned him with the news that he'd just been traded to Detroit. Sittler felt so betrayed that he vowed to quit the game rather than go to another club.

Later, during a phone conversation with Red Wings GM Jimmy Devellano, Sittler repeated his vow to retire. He urged Devellano to void the deal, calling it the biggest disappointment of his life. Sittler's wife, Wendy, broke into tears at the news. She enjoyed living in their Voorhees, New Jersey, home and dreaded a move to Detroit. Their marriage, Sittler would say later, almost came apart because of the trade.

Sittler finally decided to join the Red Wings, although he found he couldn't shake the deep depression he felt over leaving a team that was about to leap to the top of the NHL standings for one that would be hard-pressed to make the playoffs.

He also had been warned by Detroit veterans Danny Gare and his old Leaf teammate Tiger Williams that Wings coach Nick Polano would provide him with a lot more headaches. The two veterans considered Polano to be incompetent and Sittler, once he'd arrived and played a few games, was quick to agree.

The 1984–85 season was barely under way when Sittler suffered a devastating injury during a game in Toronto. Jim Korn, a huge defenseman who'd tangled with Sittler before, ran him into the boards from behind, crushing Sittler's face into the spot where the glass meets the rail, fracturing his upper cheekbone. The bone around his eye was broken in three places and the eyeball was loose in its socket. He was rushed to a nearby hospital and an operation was scheduled for the following day. Then Darryl learned that his father had suffered a heart attack while watching the game and was being monitored on another floor of the same hospital. Several weeks later the elder Sittler died.

When he recovered from the operation and returned to Detroit, Polano played Sittler on the fourth line and his ice time was cut drastically. He finished with 11 goals in 61 games and, after the Wings lost the first two games of their playoff round against Chicago, he was benched for the final game.

· After considering the unhappiness and frustration he'd felt personally and observed in those around him, he decided to meet with Devellano and clear the air. But when he stepped into the general manager's office, Devellano didn't mince words.

"Darryl, we're buying you out of your contract. You're no longer a Red Wing."

Sittler knew he was at the end of the road. He'd compiled an enviable record over his 15-season NHL career: 484 goals and 1,121 points in 1,096 games. There was the record-setting 10-point game in 1976, and late that summer he scored the winning goal in overtime against Czechoslovakia to help win the Canada Cup. But during his season in Detroit he'd produced only 27 points, his lowest total since his second year in the NHL.

Sittler's agent, Alan Eagleson, told him the Vancouver Canucks were interested in him — but for one season only. If he signed, he'd lose the salary Detroit would pay him not to play — about $260,000.

Darryl quit the game as a player and never looked back. It was time to get on with his life. He became a born-again Christian, finding great comfort in religion. He and Wendy went to counselling and put their marriage back together.

On August 8, 1991, Sittler, then 40 years old and by now a member of the Hockey Hall of Fame, rejoined the Toronto Maple Leafs after a ten-year absence, as a special consultant, a position he still holds.

Ilitch the Owner

BACK in 1959, someone told Mike Ilitch, the son of Yugoslav immigrants, not to go into the pizza business. Pizzas were just a fad. They would never catch on in a big way. It's a good thing for Ilitch — and for the Red Wings — that he ignored that advice.

One day back in '50s Ilitch persuaded a friendly bar owner in Garden City to let him set up a pizza oven on the premises. His pizzas were a hit with the patrons, and soon he was pulling in

$30 or $40 a night. It sure beat selling pots and pans door to door — one of his previous jobs — and he enjoyed being his own boss.

Ilitch was confident that his pizzas were better than others he'd sampled, so, two years later, he opened a second outlet. Then came a third and a fourth. The name over his establishments — Little Caesar's — became synonymous with good pizza and the money began to roll in.

From those humble beginnings, Little Caesar's grew into an international empire that includes over 4,500 franchised restaurants located in all 50 states, Canada, England, and Puerto Rico.

A hockey fan all his life, and a regular at Red Wings games in the '40s and '50s, Ilitch jumped at the chance to buy the team in 1982. He knew it was a sleeping giant, waiting for someone to come along and inject new life into it. And in retrospect, the $9 million price tag was a steal.

Ilitch took off his pizza apron, met with Bruce Norris, and moments later the Red Wings and their two farm clubs were his. Other acquisitions followed, including the Detroit Drive of the Arena Football League and the Detroit Tigers, one of major league baseball's most storied franchises.

During the '80s, Ilitch spent millions on fading stars such as Darryl Sittler, Tiger Williams, and Ivan Boldirev. More than $1 million went to a free-agent star from the University of Illinois-Chicago by the name of Ray Staszak, who collected one point in four NHL games. But this spectacular flop didn't curb the owner's generosity.

When John Ogrodnick scored 50 goals in 1985, Ilitch handed him a bonus of $50,000.

Steve Yzerman, Sergei Fedorov, and others were signed to multimillion-dollar contracts. Ilitch did well by his coaches too. Jacques Demers and Brad Park were the best-paid in their day, and Scotty Bowman now earns $1 million a year to guide the Red Wings.

In 1997, Ilitch disproved critics who argued that big spenders don't win championships. His Red Wings brought the Stanley Cup to Detroit for the first time since 1955.

Red Wings on a Spending Spree

IN the summer of 1985 the Red Wings sent shock waves through the hockey world with a spending spree unlike any in hockey history.

The most controversial signing was that of Pittsburgh forward Warren Young. As a 28-year-old rookie in 1984–85, Young had played on a line with Mario Lemieux and potted 40 goals. When the Wings signed him to a four-year pact said to be worth $1 million, Pittsburgh general manager Eddie Johnston accused Detroit of tampering, alleging they'd spoken to Young before he officially became a free agent on July 1.

"Don't get me wrong, I'm happy for Warren," Johnston said. "But when you are paying him twice what you are paying Steve Yzerman and as much as you are paying John Ogrodnick or Ron Duguay, there's something wrong with that organization."

Jim Lites, the Wings' executive vice-president, denied the allegations of tampering, but the charges were echoed by Minnesota GM Lou Nanne, who claimed the Red Wings had contacted veteran North Star defenseman Harold Snepsts on June 27. "Snepsts called me on that day and asked me if I'd match the Red Wings offer," he said.

Detroit management also drew flak for a round of big-ticket signings of star college players. "There are 20 general managers around the league who are totally ticked off with the Red Wings," Johnston said. "They've knocked the NHL salary structure completely out of whack. Those college kids are getting more right now than Mario Lemieux and they haven't played a game yet."

Though Detroit may have been able to shrug off such criticism, they couldn't ignore the fact that none of their college recruits made an impact in the NHL.

Chris Cichocki, a Detroit native and Michigan Tech graduate, scored 10 goals in his rookie year as a Red Wing, played in two games the next season, then was sent to New Jersey where he played in seven games over two years, scoring one goal.

Dale Krentz, a left winger form Steinbach, Manitoba, and a Michigan State grad, played in 30 games over three seasons, scoring five goals and eight points. (Cichocki and Krentz were both represented by Bob Goodenow, who went on to succeed Alan Eagleson as executive director of the NHL Players' Association.)

Tim Friday, a defenseman from Burbank, California, out of RPI, played in 23 NHL games and collected three assists.

And, of course, there was Ray Staszak, a right winger born in Philadelphia. "Ray is a Bob Nystrom–type player," said Wings GM Jimmy Devellano. By way of comparison, Nystrom played in 900 NHL games, scored 235 goals, and played on four Stanley Cup–winning teams. Staszak played four games in a Red Wing uniform, collected one assist, and was sent to Adirondack, never to return to the NHL.

Adam Oates, from Weston, Ontario, a star at RPI, had seasons of 9, 15, 14, and 16 goals with Detroit before they shipped him to St. Louis, where he topped 100 points the next two years. As a Boston Bruin he enjoyed a career high of 142 points in 1992–93. He now plays for Washington and is a career 1,000-point scorer.

As for Warren Young, he scored 22 goals and added 24 assists for 46 points during his one season in Detroit. Without Lemieux to feed him, Young was missing in action. He returned to Pittsburgh for parts of two seasons, scored eight goals in 57 games, and faded from the scene.

More About Ray Staszak

IN 1985, Ray Staszak was one of the most sought-after free agents in NHL history. Something about him made the scouts label him a "can't-miss" prospect. He seemed to have the blend of toughness — he once singlehandedly took on three thugs who were trying to steal his car — and scoring — 37 goals and 72 points in his senior year at the University of Illinois-Chicago — that coaches, scouts, and general managers dream of.

Eighteen NHL teams wanted him badly and were willing to open their vaults to land him, but the Red Wings emerged as the winning bidder, with a deal even richer than the $1.1 million they'd dished out weeks earlier for RPI star Adam Oates. Staszak got a five-year pact worth $1.3 million.

Thanks to agent Brian Burke (now a top NHL executive), the young man who paid for ice time at a Chicago rink by emptying garbage cans wouldn't have to worry about money any more.

"He can't miss," said Montreal scout André Boudrias, using the words a scout is too often prone to utter, later to wish he'd bitten his tongue.

"Every team needs a winger like Staszak," added Max McNab of the Devils.

"Bobby Hull played on the Million-Dollar Line," quipped Doug Robinson, another Hab scout. "Now Detroit has a Three-Million-Dollar Line in [Warren] Young, [Adam] Oates, and Staszak."

Jimmy Devellano said, "We put a lot of thought and planning into our signings. What we did was financially responsible." He added with a grin, "The league was so dull this summer we had to do something."

Sadly for Staszak and the Wings, it never worked out.

His NHL stats occupy one line of type in the NHL record book: four games, no goals, one assist, one point, seven penalty minutes. Not much to show for a seven-figure investment.

The Worst Hockey Team That Money Could Buy

AFTER the Red Wings finished dead last in 1985–86, writer Vartan Kupelian looked back in anger on a team that had suffered the most defeats (57) in the history of the once-proud franchise. In *The Hockey News*, Kupelian tried to explain why he'd predicted a first-place finish for the Wings before the season started:

Okay, you want reasons, I'll give you reasons. I picked the Wings to finish first right after I got hit in the head with a Reed Larson slapshot. It was sheer madness. I wanted to prove something: The Red Wings don't need help turning a silk purse into a sow's ear. There was nothing negative about the media in Detroit this season but even a ridiculously positive media couldn't rescue this most inept of all professional sports franchises. They are completely capable of being rotten without any help from us.

The Red Wings are a mess. Even they'll tell you that. "Not in my wildest nightmares would I have thought anything like this would happen," Jimmy D[evellano] said. And, as GM of hockey's worst team, it should be noted that the man is subject to some horrifying nightmares.

Remember, the product on the ice is a reflection of the organization. Plain and simple. It starts at the top. Owner Mike Ilitch indiscriminately signed untested college free agents for enormous sums of money last summer, and eight free agents in all. He tried to buy a shortcut to respectability. It led to a dead end . . . and when the Wings ignored the warning signs, they went over the cliff. The fall was long, hard, and painful.

The monumental flop of the free agents won't be a deterrent in the future. On the contrary, Ilitch promises to do it again, even spend twice as much if he has to. That ought to cheer the hearts of player agents all over the continent.

The owner then complicated matters by hiring two men — Devellano and Brad Park (coach, director of player personnel) — to do basically the same job, and all that produced was even more confusion and enmity.

(By the way, the Wings actually got worse under Park, earning 20 points in 45 games, the same number collected in 35 games with deposed coach Harry Neale.)

Clearly, the problems go beyond a dressing room full of players who don't belong in the NHL. It goes to the very underpinning of the organization, and a critical point that needs attention is the matter of who's in charge here? Right now, the Red Wings are being run by committee. And that doesn't work.

On the ice, the Wings fall short of major-league standards and only one man, Devellano, is responsible for that. He's been on the job for four years now and the product is no better than when he arrived. The question most often asked is: How much longer will Ilitch stick with Jimmy D? Only Ilitch knows. Maybe. He hasn't come up with many right answers in four yours either. All he's got so far is the worst hockey team money can buy.

Harry Neale Gets Socked

RECENTLY, basketball star Latrell Sprewell was in the news when he tried to choke his coach, P. J. Carlesimo. Sprewell was suspended for a year and his team, the Golden State Warriors, terminated the remaining three years of his $32-million contract. Later, an arbitrator ruled the dual penalties too harsh, reduced the suspension by five months, and reinstated the contract.

Does the Sprewell incident have a parallel in hockey? Harry Neale, who coached the Red Wings briefly in 1985–86, could tell you. Neale was attacked by an enraged player one night, not while he coached the sad-sack Red Wings, but when he was in charge of the New England Whalers of the World Hockey Association.

The player, tough guy Gord Gallant, missed curfew one night on a road trip. Neale made a routine call to Gallant's room and he wasn't there. But his roommate was. "Have Gord call me when he gets in," Neale told the roommate. "I'm up in room 615." Neale went to his room, took off his clothes, and prepared for bed.

The phone rang. It was Gallant's roommate with a warning: "Coach, Gord is coming up there. And he's really pissed. Better be careful."

Just as Neale put down the phone, there was a knock at the door. Harry pulled the door open and found himself staring at Gallant's big fist, headed for his face. *Pow!* Gallant then pulled his coach into the corridor and began to pummel him. Harry was naked and being thrown around like a rag doll. Harry's roommate, assistant coach Jack McCartan, raced from the room to give Harry a hand. Gallant turned his attention to McCartan and threw him back into the room, wrestling him to the floor. The door slammed shut behind them.

Awakened and disturbed by the noise, people opened doors along the corridor. Locked out of his room, Harry pounded on the door. He could hear shouts, curses, and crashing sounds from within. He pictured poor McCartan, his assistant coach, being murdered. Some Whalers arrived on the scene and took control. Somehow the door swung open and the battle inside was halted. Gallant was escorted back to his room while Neale threw on some clothes and examined the bruises to his face and the damage to his room.

There were no charges of assault, no investigation by the league, no fine, no suspension, and no police involvement. Unlike the Sprewell case, the incident didn't even make the sports pages.

In the morning, Harry Neale had his "to do" list well prepared. First he told hotel officials he'd pay for any damages.

Then he got on the phone and traded Gord Gallant.

What Fergie Says

JOHN Ferguson has been a player, coach, and manager in the NHL. He is remembered as one of the toughest players ever to perform in the NHL but his opinions are also among the most respected. Over the years he's commented on Red Wings' personnel and players.

On Brendan Shanahan: "Brendan Shanahan was a member of Team Canada in 1989 when I coached the team in the world championships. Shanahan hadn't performed all that well in his first couple of seasons with New Jersey (7 and 22 goals) but he impressed me as a kid who was beginning to put it all together. I said to him, 'Kid, one of these days you're going to be a star in this league.'"

About Steve Yzerman: "Let's compare Steve Yzerman and Mario Lemieux. I'd go with Yzerman because he's a better team player and is less outspoken. He also gets more respect from his teammates than Mario Lemieux. Unlike Mario, Stevie negotiates directly with his general manager and not in the press. Lemieux goes around saying, 'we need toughness, we need this, we need that . . .'"

On Howie Young: "I wanted to kill that bastard. And I would have killed Howie Young if I'd gotten my hands on him. I put Young way up on my list of players I despised. I always felt that he was a phoney, certainly nothing near the fighter that he was built up to be by the media."

On Gordie Howe: "Howe was the strongest, meanest player I ever met. He was by far the best 'stick man.' Once I checked him and he wrapped his stick around my mouth and ripped my tongue open with the blade. How do you check a Howe? You must stand up to him. You absolutely cannot let him think he can intimidate you. [If you do] he'll take the entire lane away from you. I could match him in physical strength and aggressiveness but we never fought."

On Jimmy Devellano: "I told a newsman once, 'Don't worry about Jimmy. He's going to build that Detroit club because he won't trade his draft choices. He'll turn that club around.' Jimmy wrote me a thank you note which I've kept to this day. He's got class. He's a good friend, a hard worker, the brains behind the Red Wings. Remember when he had the fourth pick in 1983 and went for Steve Yzerman? A monumental move for his franchise. I'll never forget one time when I wanted to made a deal with him for Ron Duguay. I thought Duguay might help Winnipeg. And Jimmy said to me, 'Fergie, you don't want Duguay. He's a dog, a fucking dog!'"

On Mike Ilitch: "Detroit is the classic example of a city whose owner remade the team in a positive way. Mike Ilitch has done wonders for the Red Wings. He has promoted [the team] well and knows how to sell everything from pizzas to Red Wing shirts."

A Valuable Franchise

T HERE are 113 major-league sports franchises operating in North America — with more coming on stream every year — and *Financial World* publishes an annual ranking of the dollar-value of each. No hockey team has cracked the top 50.

In 1998, the Chicago Blackhawks, the NHL's most valuable hockey franchise at $151 million, placed 53rd on the list. The Hawks and the New York Rangers had overtaken the Red Wings, the 1996 leader at $126 million, even though their value had grown to $146 million. The most valuable of all pro sports franchises on the 1998 survey were the Dallas Cowboys at an estimated $320 million.

Given that information, it's remarkable that, when Bruce Norris put the Red Wings up for sale in 1982, the asking price was $13 million. Mike Ilitch had already tried to buy the club for

$11 million, but his offer had been rejected. He came back later with a much lower bid — said to be around $9 million — and got the Wings, plus two minor-league affiliates, but not the Joe Louis Arena. He said, "I think the Detroit franchise is one of the best in hockey. It's a sleeping giant waiting for someone to do something with it."

Both on the ice and in the boardroom, he was absolutely right.

Motor City Moses

M OSES. That's what they called Jacques Demers when he led the Detroit Red Wings out of the hockey wilderness beginning in 1986. Growing up in Montreal, Demers was the original rink rat, a kid who sneaked into the Forum so often they finally figured he must work there. That's when he made up his mind he wanted to be a coach some day.

At 16 he lost his mother, who died of leukemia. Two years later his father died of a heart attack. As the oldest child, he took on the responsibility of looking after his two sisters and a brother. He found a job as a truck driver. He took night courses to upgrade his education. And he coached kids' hockey teams.

Then came a miraculous opportunity. Two former NHLers, Pat Stapleton and Marcel Pronovost, recommended him for a job as assistant coach with the WHA's Chicago Cougars. Along the way he worked hard at learning to speak English.

His work in Chicago attracted the attention of Maurice Filion, manager of the Quebec Nordiques, who hired Demers as his head coach for 1978–79, the final year of the WHA. Quebec won 41 games under Demers, good for second place in the six-team league. But the following year, their first in the NHL, was a bummer. They won only 25, lost 44, and finished last in their division.

During the 1979–80 season, Demers gave one young player a chance he will never forget. Farmhand Paul Stewart was called up for a game in his home town at the Boston Garden one night. Stewart told my colleague Dick Irvin, "Right away I got into a bit of a stickfight with Wayne Cashman. That was in the warmup. Then I fought Terry O'Reilly, Stan Jonathan, and Al Secord, three of the toughest Bruins. I got three majors and was thrown out of the game. But I was so excited and grateful to Demers for giving me a chance to play in my home town. Later, I knocked on his door and planted a big kiss on him. I was really sorry when they canned him at the end of the year." That was the same Paul Stewart who now referees in the NHL.

In 1983, Demers was hired by the St. Louis Blues and he moved the cash-strapped Blues from fourth place in the Norris Division to first in just two seasons. He managed to improve the team even though the club's financial future looked so shaky and the front office was so disorganized that the team did not take part in the 1983 draft. By 1986 the Blues found themselves in the Stanley Cup semifinals against Calgary. They lost the dramatic series in game seven by a 2–1 score. During the playoffs, Demers was chastised after he admitted he threw pennies on the ice during games to hold up play and give his players a chance to catch their breath.

In June 1986, Mike Ilitch opened the vault and wooed Demers to Detroit. He made the former truck driver the highest-paid coach in NHL history, signing him to a five-year, $1.1-million contract. Demers replaced Brad Park, who'd lasted only 45 games and left a parting shot directed at general manager Jimmy Devellano: "Everybody points out the mistakes I made in three months and they overlook all the mistakes Devellano made in the four years he had to make something of the Wings."

Demers became Detroit's 17th coach in 18 years. At the time, Frank Orr wrote in the *Toronto Star*: "Demers is a master of extracting the largest possible percentage of the potential from the players handed him to coach. He's tough and demanding but does it without ever forgetting that humans are involved or that the workers simply played a bad game of hockey, not the perpetration of some heinous crime against humanity."

The Leafs' "Big M," Frank Mahovlich, chases "Mr. Hockey," Gordie Howe. During the 1967–1968 season, Mahovlich was traded to Detroit, where he played on a line with Howe. — Hockey Hall of Fame

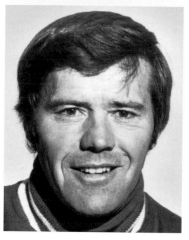

Billy Dea was to earn a contractual bonus if he scored 15 goals or more in the 1956–57 season. He scored his 15th goal on the last night of the season, but he needed help from Gordie Howe and Norm Ullman.
— Detroit Red Wings

As part of a Hockey Night in Canad[a] intermission in the 1960s, the author [is?] Santa to Gordie Howe, who's asking f[or] little more scoring help for the struggl[ing] Red Wings.   — Hockey Hall of Fame

Marcel Pronovost of the Leafs checks Alex Delvecchio. Delvecchio scored 456 goals as a Red Wing and played in 1,549 games. He won the Lady Byng Trophy three times and was elected to the Hall of Fame in 1977.   — Hockey Hall of Fame

Terry Sawchuk's goals-against average was less than two per game in each of his first five seasons as a Red Wing. He survived many serious injuries on the ice, but died in a New York hospital following an unusual off-ice incident in 1970 at the age of 40. — Hockey Hall of Fame

In this memorable photo taken at a Brantford sports banquet, "Mr. Hockey" meets the "Great One" to be, Wayne Gretzky.

— Hockey Hall of Fame

Detroit's Danny Grant, a 50-goal sco 1974–75, was a champion on the po Hockey Night in Canada *intermissi* feature *"Showdown in the NHL,"* hos by the author.   — Hockey Hall of Fame

During the 1975–76 season, goalie Jim Rutherford tied a Red Wing record set by Glenn Hall by registering three shutouts in a row. Rutherford is now the general manager of the Carolina Hurricanes.   — Hockey Hall of Fame

Dennis Polonich successfully sued Wil Paiement of the Colorado Rockies, who injured the Red Wing forward with a hockey stick. Polonich was awarded ar $850,000 settlement.   — Detroit Red W

Mike Ilitch purchased the struggling
Red Wings franchise in June 1982 for a
bargain price, and turned it into one of
the league's most respected organizations.

— Detroit Red Wings

Jimmy Devellano joined the Red Wings
as general manager on July 12, 1982.
He built a championship team through
the draft, trades, and free agency and
now serves as senior vice president.

— Detroit Red Wings

Bryan Watson was a fan favorite. According
to Leaf manager Punch Imlach, Watson,
"drove most of the best players in the game
absolutely crazy." — Detroit Red Wings

In 1997, Red Wing captain Steve Yzerman
brought the Stanley Cup to an Ottawa
arena. In an emotional moment, Yzerman
handed it to a disabled childhood friend.

— Hockey Hall of Fame

At the beginning of the 1997–98 season, Red Wing fans cheer as the 1996–97 championship banner is raised. — Hockey Hall of Fame

After parading around the arena with the Stanley Cup in 1997, goaltender Mike Vernon carried off another award — the Conn Smythe Trophy he earned as the most valuable player of the playoffs.

— Hockey Hall of Fame

Steve Yzerman, who won the 1998 Conn Smythe Trophy as playoff MVP, holds the Stanley Cup high above his head.

— Bruce Bennett

Vladimir Konstantinov, injured in an off-ice accident in 1997, takes part in the celebrations. In a touching moment, Steve Yzerman gave the Cup to Konstantinov, who made a victory lap around the ice.

— Bruce Bennett

Early on, Demers surprised the Detroit players' wives by taking them out to lunch one day, just to say "thank you for all the little things they do to help the team. It's not an easy job, being married to someone in a high-stress job like playing hockey," Demers explained. What a change from Jack Adams's day, when wives and families always came second to hockey. According to Colleen Howe, when player Billy McNeill's pregnant wife contracted polio and was hospitalized, McNeill was told he was "needed" for a game in Chicago. While he was away, his wife died. Shortly after the funeral, McNeill was traded to New York.

Under Demers, the Red Wings improved dramatically. They climbed from last place and 40 points in 1985–86 to second place in the Norris Division in 1987. They went to the semifinals the next year, and won back-to-back divisional titles in 1988 and 1989. Then, just when he figured he had his best lineup ever, in 1989–90, the Wings plummeted to last place with just 70 points.

On July 13 — a Friday the 13th — Red Wing owner Mike Ilitch stunned Detroit fans by giving the popular Demers the boot after the four best years the franchise had enjoyed since the 1960s. Bryan Murray was brought in to replace both Demers and Devellano, who was kicked upstairs to an executive position. Demers left graciously, refusing to offer excuses or take shots at the two men he was told were largely responsible for his departure — Devellano and team captain Steve Yzerman.

Demers went on to coach the 1993 Stanley Cup–winning Habs.

The Cup Comes Home

Demers Is Sacked

ON July 13, 1990, Detroit owner Mike Ilitch fired Jacques Demers, the man who had guided his Red Wings to four of the most successful years the franchise had enjoyed since the 1960s. Two days earlier, general manager Jimmy Devellano had been promoted to the position of senior vice-president of the Wings, and Bryan Murray had been signed to replace both men.

Ironically, Murray, who had been fired by Washington in January and replaced by his brother Terry, had received a phone call from Demers while he was unemployed. "I called him and told him not to be discouraged," Demers recalled. "I told him he wouldn't be out of work very long. But I didn't dream the job he would get would be mine."

Demers suspected that Devellano and — of all people — Steve Yzerman were responsible for his downfall. "I don't know for sure," he said, "but I have been told by three different people that it was Stevie who did me in during a private meeting he had with Mike Ilitch. I always included Stevie in any discussions we had about the team. He's the greatest athlete I ever coached. He never cheated, always put out on the ice, always gave me 100 percent."

Yzerman denied any involvement in the dismissal of Demers. He said he was innocent of charges he stabbed his coach in the back during a meeting with the team owner. "Sure I had a meeting with Mr. Ilitch," said Yzerman. "We talked about my contract and we talked about hockey. But he never asked me if I thought Jacques should stay or go."

Public sentiment in Detroit ran heavily in favor of Demers and against the Red Wings' brass. A *Detroit Free Press* poll of over

1,000 readers showed 61 percent were on the coach's side. A fan named Raymond Rahi wrote: "When Demers was hired the Red Wings were in shambles. In one season he managed to restore a sense of self-respect and excitement that Detroit fans had not experienced since the 1950s. He became a legend here because of the class, dignity and honesty with which he conducted himself. Sure, the Red Wings had a terrible season [70 points and fifth place in the Norris Division in 1989–90] but did Demers trade Adam Oates and Paul MacLean for Bernie Federko and Tony McKegney? Did he trade away four young players for an injured Jimmy Carson? Was he in charge of the poor scouting and drafting over the past several years? The man who must bear the blame for the misfortune of the Red Wings is former general manager Jimmy Devellano. Despite the many years of turmoil and losing, I have always been proud to be a Red Wing season ticket-holder. I am no longer proud. I am embarrassed. I am ashamed."

We Miss You, Vlad

OLDTIMERS in the town of Murmansk, north of the Arctic Circle, still talk of the convoys of merchant ships that arrived from North America during World War II, bringing supplies and weapons to the Russian people. The long winters in Murmansk, where daylight replaces darkness for only a couple of hours each day, provided ideal conditions for skating — and for hockey.

One of the best teenage hockey stars in that cold, remote place was Vladimir Konstantinov, an aggressive young defenseman and center who was recruited by the famous Red Army team in Moscow in 1984 when he was only 17. By 1989, after five years (and four world championships) he was named captain of the Red Army team.

Throughout the 1990–91 season he yearned to join country-man Sergei Fedorov in Detroit. Fedorov had defected from the Russian national team during the Goodwill Games in Seattle in July 1990. The Detroit Red Wings had drafted Konstantinov in the 11th round, 221st overall back in 1989, but his route to the NHL involved some chicanery. With the help of bribe money, certain Russian officials confirmed a report that Konstantinov had a rare form of cancer, a type that could only be treated in the United States. After much shuffling and stamping of papers, he was allowed to leave. He made the long trip to Detroit and never looked back.

Konstantinov adapted to the NHL style of play almost immediately and soon gained a reputation as one of the game's most feared and ferocious defensemen. He delivered devastating bodychecks and didn't hesitate to use his stick, when necessary, like a machete. Opposing players cursed him; opposing coaches chastised him. The newspapers dubbed him Vlad the Impaler and Bad Vlad.

Detroit fans loved him. He was named to the All-Rookie team after the 1991–92 season, and in 1995–96 he led all NHL players in plus-minus with a fabulous plus-60. His two Russian team-mates, Sergei Fedorov and Slava Fetisov, finished second and third in plus-minus, at plus-49 and plus-37 (tied with Petr Nedved of Pittsburgh). In the summer of 1996 Konstantinov underwent surgery to repair a torn Achilles tendon he suffered when he and Fedorov were playing a casual game of tennis.

The sweetest of all his seasons was 1996–97, when he helped lead the Red Wings to the coveted Stanley Cup. Once a regular visitor to Detroit, Lord Stanley's old basin hadn't been seen in Hockeytown since 1955.

After their four-game sweep of Philadelphia in the final series, the Red Wings were saluted by a million fans at a downtown rally in their honor. Konstantinov, the runner-up for the Norris Trophy, feeling the devotion of all those supporters, held the Cup aloft. "This Cup is for you, for Detroit, for Michigan," he shouted.

There was one last team function to attend before the players dispersed for the summer. On June 13 the Wings met for a golf outing, followed by a get-together at the home of Red Wing goalie Chris Osgood.

It was arranged for limousines to take the players from the golf course to the Osgood residence. Konstantinov, Fetisov, and team masseur Sergei Mnatsakanov hopped into a limo driven by Richard Gnida, whose name was soon to become almost as well known as the players he chauffered. Richard Gnida's driver's license had been revoked following several violations. He was driving his limo at about 50 miles per hour through Birmingham, Michigan, when the huge vehicle went out of control. It veered crazily across several lanes, flew over a curb, and smashed into a tree.

Later police would state that the limo's brakes had not been applied, that Gnida was found to have marijuana in his system. Presumably, he fell asleep at the wheel.

His three passengers weren't wearing seat belts — people who travel in limos seldom do. When the limo slammed into the tree, all three were thrown forward. Fetisov was the most fortunate. He struck the wet bar and was not seriously injured. But Konstantinov and Mnatsakanov struck the partition head first. It's a wonder they weren't killed instantly. Their unconscious bodies were pulled from the wreck. They were rushed to hospital suffering from severe brain trauma. Konstantinov also required an operation on his elbow and Mnatsakanov underwent spinal surgery.

It was late July before Konstantinov and Mnatsakanov began to emerge from their comas. Their injuries were no longer considered to be life-threatening. A neurosurgeon said, "We're encouraged, but we have many, many months of hard rehab ahead of us. It's too early to say anything about a full recovery."

The horrific accident ended any further Stanley Cup celebrations. Teammate Igor Larionov, a daily vistor to the hospital, said, "You see Vlad holding the Stanley Cup, so happy, so proud, so strong. And now this." He told writer Mike Nadel, "When you see a man in good shape . . . and all of a sudden he's lost 30 pounds. It's very sad. It's emotionally and physically tiring to see him there, like that, when we remember him being so strong."

Larionov was to have accompanied his mates in the limo but he had skipped the golf tournament to take his daughter swimming. "God saved me that day but I don't know why," he said.

Teammates brought the gleaming Stanley Cup into the hospital and Konstantinov's hand was placed on its surface. No one knows if he recognized it, no one knows what he felt. He and his Russian mates had planned to bring the Cup to Moscow in August. Now they would have to go without him. It would have been his first time back home. It would have been a wonderful journey.

Larionov, during his daily visits, would whisper to him in Russian. "You must be strong again, Vlad. You must come back to us. You can do it. You must."

On November 7, 1997, Richard Gnida, the limousine driver, was sentenced to nine months in jail and 15 months on probation. He was also ordered to attend Alcoholics Anonymous meetings four times a week and to get counselling. "You shattered lives," Judge Kimberly Small told Gnida. "Based on your behavior you have a serious drug and alcohol problem. And what scares me is, you don't know it." The following day, Konstantinov was able to attend a private ceremony at which the Red Wings received their Stanley Cup rings.

Yzerman Brings the Cup to Yzerman Arena

I N late August 1997, Steve Yzerman brought the Stanley Cup to Ottawa. More properly, he brought it to the suburb of Nepean, where he'd played his minor hockey and where he once led a pee-wee team to the provincial championship.

Yzerman carefully removed the Stanley Cup from the back of his white convertible and walked along the red carpet that led to a crowd of a couple of thousand people gathered in the new Steve Yzerman Arena.

In the crowd that day was another Steve — an old friend

named Steve Unger. As a teenager, Unger had shared Yzerman's love for hockey and he played the game marvelously well. Like Yzerman, he had played for the Nepean Raiders. He was a centerman who would surely become a skilled professional, a star in the NHL. Everybody said so.

But in 1984, the 16 year old went swimming at Brittania Bay, a suburb of Ottawa. He dove into the water and broke his neck, an injury that would change his life forever. The blow he suffered left him paralyzed, a quadriplegic.

Following the accident, Yzerman and former Nepean goalie Darren Pang approached several friends and acquaintances, raised some money, and set up a trust fund for their pal. Before long, Unger had a new van he could drive himself. He had a dog by his side, one who could even bring him drinks from the fridge. Unger, now 30, will be forever grateful for the generosity and the compassion shown by those around him, especially old friends and teammates who pitched in to help.

Suddenly Yzerman spotted Unger in the crowd and, without hesitating, walked over to the smiling man in the wheelchair. Gently he placed the gleaming trophy in Unger's lap. Tears welled up in Unger's eyes as the arena filled with the cheers and applause of the onlookers. Steve Yzerman, hockey superstar, and Steve Unger, who might have been one, shared a very precious moment.

Let's Call It the Ilitch Cup

WHEN the Red Wings captured Lord Stanley's prized silverware in 1997, owner Mike Ilitch had the names of his seven children engraved on hockey's most important trophy. A total of nine members of the Ilitch clan can find their names engraved on both versions of the Stanley Cup, which must be some kind of a record.

Mike Ilitch and his wife, Marian, are co-owners of the Red Wings, while their sons Atanas and Christopher are listed as vice-presidents. Also on the Cup, however, are the names of Denise Ilitch Lites, Ronald Ilitch, Michael Ilitch Jr., Lisa Ilitch Murray, and Carole Ilitch Trepeck. The ladies in the Ilitch family join the only other female names on the Cup — Marguerite Norris, who was president of the Red Wings in the 1950s, Marie DeBartolo York, president of the 1991 Penguins, and Sonia Scurfield, part-owner of the 1989 Flames.

None of the five named above was involved with the Red Wings on a full-time basis, although Ilitch spokesperson Al Sebastien maintains "all of the Ilitch children are involved in the family business in one way or another."

Red Wings in the
White House

WHEN the Stanley Cup champion Detroit Red Wings were honored at the White House in January 1998, President Bill Clinton said he was "thrilled" to be able to meet Vladimir Konstantinov, a player he said had "the heart of a champion." Clinton posed for a photo with the great Russian player, who had spent five weeks in a coma after a postseason accident on June 13, 1997. The president said the photo would heighten his popularity in Russia. "Vlad, we know how hard you've been working and how far you've come," he told the indestructible Red Wing. Konstantinov nodded his head, indicating he understood the message. He received a standing ovation from all those assembled.

Team captain Steve Yzerman — after presenting the president with a Detroit jersey emblazoned with the name CLINTON and the number 1 on the back — pointed out that the last time the Red Wings held the Stanley Cup was in 1955, when Dwight D. Eisenhower was president. "But I don't think Ike was much of a hockey fan," quipped Yzerman, "so Gordie and the boys never got an invite to the White House."

When coach Scotty Bowman presented the president with a replica of the Stanley Cup, Mr. Clinton told him, "Scotty, you've won this trophy so many times they should call it the Stanley Bowman Cup."

Hockey News on Howe

W HEN Gordie Howe announced he would make a blink-of-an-eye comeback with the Detroit Vipers of the International Hockey League in 1997, *Hockey News* editor Steve Dryden offered these observations:

> *The Hockey News* and our agents have been among the harshest critics of the Gordie Howe (and why) sixth-decade appearance.
>
> Now let us be equally firm in another position: Howe's aborted quest for a single shift with the Syracuse Crunch and eventual second skate with the Detroit Vipers on October 3 does nothing, absolutely nothing, to tarnish the legend.
>
> When you think of Howe in the years to come — and you will — do not be distracted from the wonder of a career never to be equaled. If he's not the best player of all-time, he is certainly the most resilient.
>
> His stop-and-start career was stunning.
>
> To emerge from retirement after a fabulous NHL career, play six seasons in the World Hockey Association (averaging more than a point a game) and then score 15 goals as a

51 year old in the NHL defies the laws of science. As Howe rang up a 96-point season the year he turned 50, he didn't belong in the uniform of the New England Whalers as much as he belonged in the pages of the *New England Journal of Medicine*.

That Howe continues to profit from his name in some curious promotions may be distasteful and vaudevillian, but he is entitled to earn a living as he sees fit, and nothing he does now should have any impact on how he is remembered. Fans and myth-makers alike love their heroes to be smudge-proof and just as heroic off the playing field as on it. Joe DiMaggio remains the archetypical sporting legend because he has remained as distant and imperial in private life as he was in public life.

Fans of all ages and professions have no right to expect that from others.

When I think of Gordie Howe in his post-playing days, I will think of a leader in the monumental pension fight. I will think of each second of a shift I opposed as likely representing one year of a playing career stretching from early childhood to the elongated one he fashioned.

I will think of Wayne Gretzky earning more assists in his career than Howe did points as a dual celebration of Number 99's other-worldly talents and Number 9's prodigious point total. I will think of a man unable to accept the fact his scoring records have not been unbeatable after all, but I will not think the legend of Mr. Hockey has been sullied.

He has earned that title.

Sam Jones Holds Out

SAM Jones is a pet name for one of Detroit's brightest stars. Do you know who he is?

In 1997, free-agent center Sergei Fedorov began complaining that the standards for Russian players were different from those of players from other nations. "Things would be different around here if my name was Sam Jones," he said. So, in 1997–98, when Fedorov was a holdout for several weeks, his mates seldom talked about him in glowing terms, and when they did they referred to him as "Sam Jones." Even fellow Russian Slava Kozlov picked up on it. "Sam Jones is in Moscow," he would say, "and Sam Jones is losing a lot of money." At the time it was estimated that Sam/Sergei was losing $25,000 per day.

By February 1998, still unsigned, Sam Jones urged general manager Ken Holland to get on with a trade. He told *The Detroit News*: "There are too many issues why it will not work for me or the Red Wings. But make sure it's clear the second reason is the money. It's not the first."

Asked if he would sign with Detroit if the club offered him $10 million, he said, "No, it's not just about money."

It certainly wasn't money that enticed him to join the Russian Olympic team that played at Nagano. The Olympic experience gave Fedorov an opportunity to perform at the highest level as well as to converse with other Russians. He could find out if they agreed with his Detroit teammates (Larionov, Fetisov, and Kozlov) who chastised him for not returning to Russia with the Stanley Cup a few months earlier.

After the Olympics, Jim Rutherford, a former Red Wing goalie and now general manager of the Carolina Hurricanes, made a stunning pitch for Fedorov. Rutherford signed the restricted free agent to a six-year, $28-million offer sheet. If the Wings failed to match the offer, they would receive five first-round draft choices from Carolina. Peter Karmanos, owner of the Hurricanes, could easily afford to make such an offer. His software company, Compuware, is valued at over $7 billion.

On February 26, the Red Wings matched the Carolina offer. It called for a signing bonus of $14 million, plus $2 million in salary and the potential for Fedorov to make an additional $12 million by the summer of 1998. As it turned out, the Russian star earned the extra $12 million when the Red Wings made the conference finals. He ended up receiving $28 million for less than six months work, which has to be some kind of short-term record.

One of the first things Fedorov did on his return was try to patch up any hard feelings his teammates may have harbored toward him. He invited them all to dinner during a road trip in Phoenix — at a cost of $11,000. There are many players in the Hall of Fame whose salary for a year equaled the cost of that meal.

Maltby Blasts Cherry

WHEN left winger Kirk Maltby scored his first career hat trick against the Toronto Maple Leafs in a December 27, 1997, game at Maple Leaf Gardens, he received congratulations all around — but not from CBC commentator Don Cherry in the "Coach's Corner." Cherry blasted Maltby for not duking it out with Leaf center Steve Sullivan after an altercation, and for wearing a face shield. Perhaps Cherry didn't know that Maltby had suffered a ruptured retina and scratched cornea after taking a stick in the eye from teammate Louis Debrusk when both were Edmonton Oilers.

"Personally, I don't give (expletive deleted) what Don Cherry says about anything," Maltby growled when told of the criticism. "He puts on a show to keep his audience. If he doesn't like the way I play, too bad."

A Glaring Omission

I N 1998, *The Hockey News* went to great expense to compile a list of the Top 50 NHLers of all time.

There was a notable omission from the list, a player closing in on 600 goals and 1,500 points. That player is Steve Yzerman.

Jared Story, a fan from Grandview, Manitoba, wrote: "I would like to know why Jaromir Jagr is on the list and Steve Yzerman is not. Jagr is one of the best players ever to play the game, but Stevie Y is a far better player. Since he joined the Detroit Red Wings, they have missed the playoffs only twice. Yzerman won the Cup in 1997, has made the Canadian Olympic Team, and led the Wings to the finals in 1995. Jagr has won two Cups but Mario Lemieux was the reason for that."

Mike Sponarski of Windsor, Ontario, agreed. "How *The Hockey News* could put Jaromir Jagr on your Top 50 list and omit Steve Yzerman is beyond comprehension. Not many players have played the game with the passion and class that Stevie Y has shown. Prior to adapting his game and becoming a premier defensive player, he put up outstanding numbers while, for many years, playing on a sub-par team. What is Jagr going to do in the post-Mario years?"

If Yzerman was disappointed at not making the Top 50 list, he hid it well. And he was in good company. Mike Gartner, who will probably wind up third on the NHL's all-time goal-scoring list, didn't make it either. Nor did great goaltenders Bernie Parent or Grant Fuhr.

1997 Cup Memories

I T could be argued that Ted Lindsay was the first team captain ever to circle the ice holding the Stanley Cup aloft. It happened so long ago — in 1955 — that few Detroit fans remember it. So it was a joy to see Steve Yzerman repeat the ritual to a thunderous ovation, on June 7, 1997, at the Joe Louis Arena. Yzerman, a five time 50-goal scorer, scored goals in three games of the four-game final against Philadelphia and was runner-up in the voting for the Conn Smythe Trophy as playoff MVP. "What I've learned," he would say, "is that there is the Stanley Cup winner and then there's everyone else. We've been everyone else."

Yzerman was referring to five bleak years during which the team he captained had suffered major disappointments. In 1993 Detroit lost in the first round against the Toronto Maple Leafs. The following year there was another first-round loss — this time to the San Jose Sharks, a club that produced almost 100 fewer goals and 18 fewer points than the Red Wings. In 1995 there was the Cup sweep by the New Jersey Devils after the Wings had recorded more wins and points than any other team during the lockout-shortened season. In 1996, following a league-record 62 wins and 131 points, there was an agonizing loss to Colorado in the Western Conference finals.

In 1994 Joey Kocur helped the Rangers end 54 years of misery as a member of the 1994 Cup winners. Two years later, Kocur was traded to Vancouver, where he played in seven games. In 1996–97 there was a brief stint in the IHL with San Antonio. After that, it was midnight hockey in a beer league at a Lakeland, Michigan, rink — no hitting, no slapshots, no cheap shots. Ask anybody, and they'd have told you Kocur's 12-year career was over — done like dinner, as Tiger Williams used to say.

Then came a call in December 1996 from Scotty Bowman. Would Kocur come and help out?

Would he? The veteran almost jumped out of his skin getting to Joe Louis Arena. He played on a line with grinders Kirk Maltby and Kris Draper, and their aggressive style drove playoff opponents to distraction.

Know of a Stanley Cup drought that needs ending? Kocur's your man. He helped break strings of 54 and 42 years. Maybe his next stop should be Chicago — they haven't won the Cup since 1961. Meanwhile, his buddies in the beer league claim, "We taught the guy everything he knows."

Chris Osgood started 47 games during the 1996–97 season, posting a 23–13–9 record. He oozed confidence just before the 1997 playoffs. Fans and family called to wish him good luck. They promised they'd be rooting for him. But Osgood only played 47 minutes in those playoffs. Scotty Bowman had decided to go with 34-year-old Mike Vernon in the postseason, and Vernon responded brilliantly in 20 remarkable games, winning 16, losing only 4. His playoff goals-against average was a scintillating 1.76 and he carried away the Conn Smythe Trophy as outstanding player in the playoffs. He also earned a less-publicized reward. By winning the Cup, he fulfilled a clause in his contract that guaranteed him another season at $2.3 million. Despite the heroics, Vernon would collect that salary elsewhere. He was traded to the San Jose Sharks in August 1997 for a couple of draft choices after the Red Wings had decided Osgood and Kevin Hodson were ready for prime time.

On May 22, 1997, in game four of the Wings' bruising conference final series with Colorado, the Red Wings were up 6–0 when Avalanche coach Marc Crawford suddenly went ballistic. He lashed out verbally at Scotty Bowman, accused him of sending thugs on the ice, and appeared ready to scale the glass and invade the Detroit bench before he was restrained. His tantrum did not go unnoticed and he was fined $10,000.

There he was, age 63, out on the ice with his champions, celebrating his seventh Stanley Cup by doing what the players do, hoisting that lovely old Cup over his head, savoring the moment of triumph. "I always wanted to know what it felt like to skate around with the Cup," Scotty Bowman said, grinning broadly. Bowman became the first coach to win the Cup with three NHL clubs — Montreal, Pittsburgh, and Detroit. In four seasons behind the Detroit bench, Bowman has seen his troops assemble a winning percentage of .667, finish first in goals-against average, and set single-season records for wins and points. Their single best accomplishment was held high over his head.

Darren McCarty's huge goal came suddenly and dramatically in game four of the final series. McCarty, the Burnaby, B.C., native, drove in over the Flyer blueline with defenseman Janne Niinimaa blocking his route to the net. McCarty unveiled a nifty inside-out move that left Niinimaa gasping. He wheeled in front of Ron Hextall and tucked the puck in the corner of the net. It gave Detroit a 2–0 lead midway through the second period and the Flyers appeared to wilt visibly.

During his last days with Toronto, easy-going veteran defenseman Larry Murphy had been booed out of Maple Leaf Gardens. "Get rid of the bum," was one of the nicer things they said about him. And how they laughed when Murphy was picked up by Detroit. "Good riddance," they roared. But the laughter stopped when Murphy, teamed with the incredibly talented Nicklas Lidstrom, played the entire four-game final as if he was the reincarnation of Doug Harvey. The Flyers were stymied by the duo and failed to score a single goal when they were on the ice.

1998 Cup Triumph
Dedicated to Konstantinov

IT was an emotional and extraordinary part of Stanley Cup history, a moment that brought lumps to the throats of millions. It was not the Cup win itself, but the sight of Red Wing captain Steve Yzerman accepting the Stanley Cup and gently placing the gleaming trophy in the lap of wheelchair-bound teammate Vladimir Konstantinov. With teammates Igor Larionov and Slava Fetisov pushing his wheelchair, Konstantinov, wearing his Detroit jersey and smiling broadly, took the traditional victory lap around the MCI Center in Washington.

"I was going to give the Cup to Chris Osgood," Yzerman said later. "But Brendan Shanahan told me that Vladdy was going to be wheeled out after the game. There was no question that he deserved to be the first to hold it."

"Vlad wore No. 16 and we got 16 wins for him," said Fetisov.

The moment spoke volumes about the state of the game and the playoffs. Never before had a Stanley Cup ceremony upstaged the game, or even the series.

Scotty Bowman declined to say whether he would come back for 1998–1999 to try for a record-breaking ninth Cup win. Steve Yzerman, however, has no doubts about his future. Says the 33-year-old center, "I've played 15 seasons and I'm aiming for 20. I'm having the greatest time in my life, and I can't possibly think of not playing now."

Forty-year-old Slava Fetisov admits he's close to the end of his hockey career. He says he'll savor his time as a Red Wing and shrug off his unpleasant years as a New Jersey Devil, where he withstood slurs from opponents and teammates. Some called him a "Russian commie."

After two consecutive Cup wins, both by sweeps, dare we think of this team in terms of a dynasty? Why not? This club could end the century and open the millennium as Stanley Cup champions.

Red Wings Rewarded for Excellence

GORDIE HOWE tops the Detroit list of individual trophy winners in the NHL with six Art Ross Trophies and six Hart Trophies. Here are the Red Wings who've captured league honors over the years.

Lady Byng Memorial Trophy
(sportsmanship and gentlemanly conduct)

Marty Barry — 1937
Bill Quackenbush — 1949
Red Kelly — 1951, 1953, 1954
Earl Reibel — 1956
Alex Delvecchio — 1959, 1966, 1969
Marcel Dionne — 1975

— George Hay was runner-up to Frank Boucher in 1928
— Marty Barry was runner-up to Clint Smith in 1939
— Syd Howe was runner-up to Bill Mosienko in 1945
— Red Kelly was runner-up to Edgar Laprade in 1950 and
   to Sid Smith in 1952
— Earl Reibel was runner-up to Andy Hebenton in 1957
— Norm Ullman was runner-up to Red Kelly in 1961
— Alex Delvecchio was runner-up to Bobby Hull in 1965

James Norris Memorial Trophy
(best defenseman)

Red Kelly — 1954
Paul Coffey — 1995

— **Red Kelly** was runner-up to Doug Harvey in 1955 and in 1957
— **Marcel Pronovost** was runner-up to Doug Harvey in 1961
— **Vladimir Konstantinov** was runner-up to Brian Leetch in 1997

Hart Memorial Trophy
(most valuable player to his team)

Ebbie Goodfellow — 1940
Sid Abel — 1949
Gordie Howe — 1952, 1953, 1957, 1958, 1960, 1963
Sergei Fedorov — 1994

— **Red Kelly** was runner-up to Al Rollins in 1954
— **Gordie Howe** was runner-up to Andy Bathgate in 1959
— **Norm Ullman** was runner-up to Bobby Hull in 1965

Vezina Trophy
(best goaltender)

Norm Smith — 1937
Johnny Mowers — 1943
Terry Sawchuk — 1952, 1953, 1955

— **Alex Connell** was runner-up to Charlie Gardiner in 1932
— **John Roach** was runner-up to Tiny Thompson in 1933
— **Wilf Cude** was runner-up to Charlie Gardiner in 1934
— **Johnny Mowers** was runner-up to Turk Broda in 1941
— **Harry Lumley** was runner-up to Bill Durnan in 1945, 1949, and 1950, and to Turk Broda in 1948
— **Terry Sawchuk** was runner-up to Al Rollins in 1951 and to Harry Lumley in 1954
— **Glenn Hall** was runner-up to Jacques Plante in 1956 and 1957
— **Roger Crozier** was runner-up to Terry Sawchuk and Johnny Bower (shared) in 1965
— **Chris Osgood** was runner-up to Jim Carey in 1996

Art Ross Trophy
(leading point scorer)

Ted Lindsay — 1950
Gordie Howe — 1951, 1952, 1953, 1954, 1957, 1963

— Ebbie Goodfellow was runner-up to Howie Morenz in 1931
— Syd Howe (St.L./Det.) was runner-up to Charlie Conacher in 1935
— Marty Barry was runner-up to Dave Schriner in 1936
— Ted Lindsay was runner-up to Gordie Howe in 1952, 1953, and 1957
— Gordie Howe was runner-up to Jean Beliveau in 1956
— Norm Ullman was runner-up to Stan Mikita in 1965
— Sergei Fedorov was runner-up to Wayne Gretzky in 1994

Calder Memorial Trophy
(top rookie)

Carl Voss — 1933
Jimmy McFadden — 1948
Terry Sawchuk — 1951
Glenn Hall — 1956
Roger Crozier — 1965

— Bucko McDonald was runner-up to Mike Karakas in 1936
— Johnny Mowers was runner-up to Johnny Quilty in 1941
— Jimmy Conacher was runner-up to Howie Meeker in 1947
— Earl Reibel was runner-up to Camille Henry in 1954
— Murray Oliver was runner-up to Bill Hay in 1960
— Doug Barkley was runner-up to Kent Douglas in 1963
— Bert Marshall was runner-up to Brit Selby in 1966
— Mike Foligno was runner-up to Ray Bourque in 1980
— Steve Yzerman was runner-up to Tom Barrasso in 1984
— Sergei Fedorov was runner-up to Ed Belfour in 1991
— Nicklas Lidstrom was runner-up to Pavel Bure in 1992

Frank J. Selke Trophy
(best defensive forward)

Sergei Fedorov — 1996

— Sergei Fedorov was runner-up to Guy Carbonneau in 1992

Conn Smythe Trophy
(playoff MVP)

Roger Crozier — 1966
Mike Vernon — 1997

Lester Patrick Trophy
(for outstanding service to hockey in the U.S.)

Jack Adams — 1966 (awarded posthumously)
Gordie Howe — 1967
Alex Delvecchio — 1974
Bruce A. Norris — 1976
Mike Ilitch — 1991

Bill Masterton Trophy
(for perseverence, sportsmanship, and dedication to hockey)

Brad Park — 1984

Lester B. Pearson Award
(outstanding performer selected by the NHLPA)

Steve Yzerman — 1989
Sergei Fedorov — 1994

Jack Adams Award
(coach of the year)

Bobby Kromm — 1978
Jacques Demers — 1987, 1988

THE RED WINGS
THROUGH THE YEARS

1926–27 DETROIT IS GRANTED AN NHL FRANCHISE on September 25, 1926. Team owners sign players from the Victoria Cougars of the Western Canada Hockey League and adopt the Cougars nickname. During its inaugural season the team plays all of its 22 home games in another country at the Border Cities Arena in Windsor, Ontario. The Cougars finish in last place with a 12–28–4 record. Team records for fewest wins (12) and fewest points (28) still stand.

1927–28 JACK ADAMS ARRIVES. The Olympia, on West Grand Avenue, designed by Charles Howard Crane, becomes the new home of the Cougars. On November 22, the Cougars lose their home opener to Ottawa by a 2–1 score. Johnny Sheppard scores the lone Cougar goal.

1928–29 CALGARY NATIVE HERB LEWIS is purchased from a Duluth team for the bargain price of $5,000. He plays 11 seasons with Detroit and is inducted into the Hockey Hall of Fame in 1989. Detroit makes the first of 47 playoff appearances. Carson Cooper (18–9–27) finishes in a third-place tie with the Habs' Howie Morenz and Andy Blair of the Leafs in the scoring race. Team record for fewest goals for (72) and against (63) still stand.

1929–30 Ebbie Goodfellow breaks in with Detroit. The team is now called the Falcons, and wins only 14 of 44 games.

1930–31 EBBIE GOODFELLOW (48 points) finishes second to Howie Morenz (51 points) in the scoring race. Defenseman Harvey Rockburn sets a league record for penalty minutes with 118. The team wins 16 of 44 games, finishes fourth in American Division.

1931–32 EBBIE GOODFELLOW leads the team in goals (14), assists (16), and points (30). The third-place Falcons are eliminated by Montreal Maroons in semifinals.

1932–33 AMERICAN INDUSTRIALIST JAMES NORRIS purchases the Detroit franchise and changes the team name to the Red Wings. The team's new logo, a winged wheel, inspired by the old Montreal AAA team, strikes Norris as being a natural for a club representing the Motor City. Detroit purchases goaltender John Ross Roach from New York for $11,000 and Roach is named to the NHL's All-Star team.

1933–34 THE RED WINGS WIN the American Division title and reach the Stanley Cup finals for the first time. They bow to Chicago 3–1 in a best-of-five series.

1934–35 EBBIE GOODFELLOW HAS six penalty shot chances during the season and scores on only one. Initially, penalty shots were taken from inside a ten-foot circle a distance of 38 feet from the goal. After Ralph (Scotty) Bowman of St. Louis becomes the first player to score on a penalty shot, he is purchased by Detroit, along with Syd Howe, for $50,000. Howe finishes second to Charlie Conacher (57–47) in the individual scoring race and sparkles for the next 11 seasons in a Red Wing uniform. Larry Aurie finishes third in scoring, Herb Lewis sixth.

1935–36 MARTY BARRY FINISHES SECOND in league scoring to Sweeney Schriner (45–40). Red Wing rookie Modere (Mud) Bruneteau scores a goal in the sixth overtime period against the Montreal Maroons to end hockey's longest game. Ebbie Goodfellow has two more penalty shots and misses on both. The Red Wings win their first Stanley Cup, defeating Toronto in the finals three games to one.

1936–37 THE RED WINGS SELL GOALIE Turk Broda to Toronto for $8,000. The Wings finish in first place and repeat as Stanley Cup champions. Goalie Earl Robertson, filling in for injured Normie Smith, plays brilliantly in the finals against New York. The Red Wings win in five games. Marty Barry and Larry Aurie finish third and fourth in league scoring.

1937–38 EARL ROBERTSON IS SOLD to the New York Americans. The Red Wings win only 12 games, fall to last place in the American Division, and miss the playoffs.

1938–39 JACK ADAMS PURCHASES TWO aging super-stars — Charlie Conacher from Toronto for a reported $16,000, and 33-year-old Boston goaltender Tiny Thompson for $15,000. Conacher scores only 8 goals. The Red Wings are one of six teams in the seven-team league to make the playoffs. They oust Montreal, then lose to Toronto in the semifinals two games to one.

1939–40 THE RED WINGS FINISH in fifth place, win the first playoff round over the Americans (2–1) but lose to Toronto 2–0 in the semifinals. Ebbie Goodfellow, a defenseman, becomes the first Detroit player to win the Hart Trophy.

1940–41 JOHNNY MOWERS REPLACES Tiny Thompson in the Detroit goal. Ebbie Goodfellow is appointed playing coach. A special night is held for Jack Adams, who celebrates his 14th season with the Red Wings. Syd Howe is one of five players who finish in a second-place tie in the scoring race — all with 44 points. Boston's Bill Cowley tallies 62. Boston beats Detroit in four straight games in the Stanley Cup finals, a playoff first.

1941–42 DON GROSSO AND SID ABEL FINISH third and fifth respectively in the scoring race. Detroit ousts Montreal and Boston in the playoffs and are leading Toronto 3–0 in games in the finals when Toronto storms back to capture the series. In the first game of the Boston series, 13,525 jam the Olympia, the largest crowd ever to attend a hockey game in Detroit.

1942–43 THE RED WINGS FINISH ATOP the NHL with 61 points. Johnny Mowers wins the Vezina Trophy with a 2.48 goals-against average. The Red Wings meet the Bruins in the Stanley Cup finals and, paced by Carl Liscombe and Sid Abel, capture the Cup in four straight games.

1943–44 GOALIE NORM SMITH is committed to a wartime job in Detroit and plays home games only. Jimmy Franks is engaged to play the road games. Jack Adams soon scraps this arrangement and signs Connie Dion to play all the games. Dion wins his first six starts, including a 15–0 shutout of New York. Syd Howe scores six goals when Detroit wallops New York 12–2 in February. The Red Wings finish second, 25 points behind Montreal. They lose to Chicago 4–1 in a best-of-seven semifinal series.

1944–45 GOALTENDER CONNIE DION is replaced by Harry Lumley. A young left winger, Ted Lindsay, joins the Red Wings. A January 18th home game with New York begins at 11:13 p.m. when the Rangers are delayed by inclement weather. Detroit eliminates Boston in a seven-game semifinal series. Carl Liscombe scores four times in the Wings' 5–3 victory in game seven. The Red Wings are shut out in the first three games of the finals against Toronto, then win three in a row, only to lose game seven by a 2–1 score.

1945–46 RED WINGS JACK STEWART, Adam Brown, and Harry Watson return to the lineup after serving in the armed forces. The Wings finish in fourth place and lose to Boston in the Stanley Cup semifinals 4–1.

1946–47 ROOKIE RIGHT WINGER GORDIE HOWE makes his NHL debut with the Red Wings and scores seven goals in 58 games. Adams decides to play Howe on a line with Lindsay and Abel. The Wings' Billy Taylor sets a record with seven assists in a game and finishes third in league scoring. Toronto ousts Detroit in the semifinals 4–1.

1947–48 THE RED WINGS TRADE BILLY TAYLOR to Boston for Bep Guidolin. Detroit's new Production Line of Lindsay, Abel, and Howe helps eliminate the Rangers in the Stanley Cup semifinals, but the Red Wings lose four straight to Toronto in the finals.

1948–49 DETROIT WINS THE NHL regular-season title with 75 points, nine more than Boston. Sid Abel wins the Hart Trophy. Bill Quackenbush becomes the first defenseman to win the Lady Byng Trophy. Detroit eliminates Montreal in seven games in the semifinals only to lose four straight to Toronto in the finals.

1949–50 DETROIT WINS THE REGULAR-SEASON title with 88 points, 11 more than second place Montreal. Ted Lindsay wins the scoring crown with 78 points — nine more than Sid Abel, 10 more than Gordie Howe. The Red Wings eliminate Toronto in seven games in the semifinals and win the Stanley Cup over New York in seven games. Pete Babando scores the winning goal in the second overtime period of game seven.

1950–51 PRIOR TO THE 1950–51 SEASON Jack Adams engineers the biggest trade in NHL history, sending Harry Lumley, Al Dewsbury, Don Morrison, Jack Stewart, and Pete Babando to Chicago in return for Bob Goldham, Metro Prystai, Gaye Stewart, and Jim Henry. Red Wings become the first NHL club with more than 100 points in a season, finishing with 101. Gordie Howe wins his first Art Ross Trophy with 86 points, 20 more than runner-up Rocket Richard. Red Wings lose to Montreal 4–2 in the semifinals. Terry Sawchuk wins the Calder Trophy as rookie of the year.

1951–52 RED WINGS FINISH FIRST with 100 points. Gordie Howe captures his second straight scoring title with another 86-point season. Ted Lindsay is runner-up with 69. Jack Adams says this club is "the greatest hockey team ever assembled" after it wins eight straight playoff games to take the Stanley Cup.

1952–53 SID ABEL LEAVES TO BECOME player–coach of the Chicago Blackhawks. James Norris dies and his daughter Marguerite becomes president of the Wings. Gordie Howe wins his third straight scoring crown with a league-record 95 points. Ted Lindsay is runner-up with 71. Wings are upset by Boston in the Stanley Cup semifinals. Terry Sawchuk wins the Vezina Trophy for the second year in a row.

1953–54 ROOKIE EARL REIBEL JOINS the Production Line with Lindsay and Howe. Howe captures his fourth straight scoring title with 81 points. Wings clinch their sixth straight league title and win the Stanley Cup in a seven-game battle with Montreal on Tony Leswick's deflected shot off Doug Harvey's glove. Red Kelly is the first winner of the James Norris Trophy, awarded to the NHL's top defenseman.

1954–55 TED LINDSAY IS GIVEN a ten-day suspension for striking a spectator with his stick. Red Wings finish in first place for the seventh consecutive time. Following the famous Richard Riot in Montreal, Detroit wins the Stanley Cup by defeating Montreal in finals. Terry Sawchuk wins his third Vezina Trophy in four years.

1955–56 ADAMS TRADES TERRY SAWCHUK, Vic Stasiuk, and Marcel Bonin to Boston. Gordie Howe becomes the third player in history to surpass 300 goals. Lindsay becomes the highest scoring left winger in history, passing Aurel Joliat, when he scores his 271st goal. Montreal snaps Detroit's string of first-place finishes. Jean Beliveau wins the scoring title over Gordie Howe and leads the Habs to a five-game triumph over Detroit in the Cup finals. Detroit's Glenn Hall wins the Calder Trophy.

1956–57 DETROIT BACK ON TOP OF THE NHL standings, edging Montreal 88–82. It's their eighth title in nine years. Gordie Howe wins his fifth scoring crown, edging Ted Lindsay 89–85. Boston upsets Detroit in the semifinals, four games to one.

1957–58 IN THE OFF SEASON, TED LINDSAY and Glenn Hall are traded to Chicago. Lindsay says the new NHL Players' Association will sue the league for $3 million. Detroit players vote not to support Lindsay and the Association. Terry Sawchuk is reacquired from Boston. Detroit loses four straight to Montreal in the semifinals.

1958–59 RED WINGS DROP FROM FIRST to worst in just two seasons, finishing last for the first time since 1938, when they trailed in the league's American Division. The last time they finished last overall was in 1927, their first season.

1959–60 JACK ADAMS TRADES RED KELLY and Billy McNeill to New York for Bill Gadsby and Eddie Shack. Kelly refuses to report, is suspended, and later is traded to Toronto for Marc Reaume. Kelly helps Toronto eliminate fourth-place Detroit in the semifinals. Terry Sawchuk says the goalie facemask, introduced by Montreal's Jacques Plante on November 1, "won't last." On January 16, 1960, Howe overtakes Maurice Richard as the league's all-time scoring champ with his 947th career point. Howe wins his fifth Hart Trophy — his third in four years.

1960–61 DETROIT CONTINUES TO STRUGGLE, finishing in fourth place, 26 points back of first-place Montreal. The Wings upset Toronto (24 points better) in the semifinals but lose to Chicago in six games in the finals.

1961–62 JACK ADAMS ACQUIRES BILL GADSBY from New York for Les Hunt. Gordie Howe plays in his 1000th regular-season game and, on March 14, he scores his 500th career goal. The Wings fall back to fifth place and miss the playoffs. Jack Adams is pushed into retirement, succeeded as manager by former Wing Sid Abel.

1962–63 JACK ADAMS BECOMES PRESIDENT of the Central Pro Hockey League. After experimenting with a mask for a couple of years in practice, Terry Sawchuk decides to wear one full-time. Alex Delvecchio is named Detroit captain. Manager Sid Abel appoints Gordie Howe as assistant coach. Howe wins the Art Ross Trophy as NHL scoring leader for sixth time. Wings finish in fourth place, and lose to Toronto in finals.

1963–64 THE RED WINGS ACQUIRE GOALTENDER Roger Crozier from Chicago for problem player Howie Young. On November 10, Gordie Howe scores his 545th career goal against Montreal, breaking Rocket Richard's record. Red Wings lose the dramatic seven-game Cup final series to Toronto. Leaf defenseman Bobby Baun scores the overtime winner in game six while playing on a cracked anklebone. Terry Sawchuk breaks George Hainsworth's NHL record with his 95th shutout.

1964–65 TED LINDSAY COMES OUT OF RETIREMENT and scores 14 goals. Goalie Terry Sawchuk, left unprotected in the preseason waiver draft, is claimed by Toronto. The Red Wings finish in first place, the first time since 1957. Norm Ullman finishes second to Chicago's Stan Mikita, 87–83, in the scoring race. Roger Crozier wins the Calder Trophy. The Wings lose to third-place Chicago in the semifinals.

1965–66 TED LINDSAY RETIRES AGAIN. Wings acquire Andy Bathgate, Billy Harris, and Gary Jarrett from Toronto for Marcel Pronovost, Autry Erickson, Eddie Joyal, Larry Jeffrey, and Lowell McDonald. Gordie Howe scores his 600th goal and Lady Byng Trophy winner Alex Delvecchio tallies goal number 300. Doug Barkley is forced to retire when he suffers a detached retina. The Red Wings lose to Montreal in six games in the Cup finals. Roger Crozier wins the Conn Smythe Trophy as playoff MVP. Jack Adams is named first winner of the Lester Patrick Trophy, "for outstanding service to hockey in the United States."

1966–67 BOBBY HULL ATTACKS PESKY Red Wing checker Bryan Watson, and cuts him for 18 stitches. Gordie Howe becomes the second winner of the Lester Patrick Trophy. Norm Ullman finishes third and Gordie Howe is fifth in the scoring race. Detroit misses the playoffs with a fifth-place finish.

1967–68 DETROIT IS MOVED TO THE EAST DIVISION of the expanded NHL. The Wings send Norm Ullman, Paul Henderson, and Floyd Smith to Toronto for Frank Mahovlich, Garry Unger, Pete Stemkowski, and the rights to Carl Brewer. The Wings finish sixth in the East. Only the Oakland Seals have a worse record. In May 1968, Jack Adams dies of a heart attack at age 72.

1968–69 GORDIE HOWE RECORDS HIS FIRST (and only) 100-point season in the NHL, finishing third in the scoring race with 103. Howe, Delvecchio, and Mahovlich set a record for goals as a line with 118 but the Wings finish fifth in the East, out of the playoffs again. Delvecchio wins his third Lady Byng Trophy. Terry Sawchuk plays 13 games in his third tour of duty with Detroit.

1969–70 BILL GADSBY IS REPLACED AS COACH by Sid Abel. Abel, team owner Bruce Norris, and Red Kelly are inducted into the Hockey Hall of Fame. Carl Brewer joins the team after a four-year absence from the NHL and (briefly) becomes the highest-paid Red Wing. Gordie Howe scores his 800th goal (counting regular season and playoffs). Alex Delvecchio becomes the third player in history to score 1,000 career points. After finishing third with 95 points, the Wings lose to the Blackhawks in the first round of the playoffs.

1970–71 BILL GADSBY IS INDUCTED INTO the Hockey Hall of Fame. New coach Ned Harkness moves Gordie Howe back to defense. Carl Brewer re-retires after one season. Sid Abel feuds with Harkness and resigns as GM. Harkness takes his place. The Red Wings finish last in their division. Gordie Howe, with 786 goals in 25 years, ends his career as a Red Wing. Detroit finishes seventh in the East, behind first-year expansion clubs Buffalo and Vancouver.

1971–72 JOHNNY WILSON TAKES OVER as Detroit coach, replacing Doug Barkley. Terry Sawchuk is inducted posthumously into the Hall of Fame. The Wings finish in fifth place in the East Division.

1972–73 ON JANUARY 28, DETROIT ROOKIE Henry Boucha sets a record by scoring a goal just six seconds after the opening face-off of a game at Montreal. Alex Delvecchio becomes the second-leading career point scorer behind Gordie Howe. Mickey Redmond is the first Red Wing to top 50 goals in a season with 52. The Wings finish in fifth place, and miss the playoffs by two points.

1973–74 ALEX DELVECCHIO ENDS HIS 24-YEAR PLAYING career, and replaces Ted Garvin as coach. Ned Harkness resigns as GM after the 1973–74 season, ending a turbulent four-year career. Detroit finishes in sixth place in the East Division. Gordie Howe and sons Mark and Marty make their debut with the Houston Aeros of the WHA.

1974–75 MARCEL DIONNE BREAKS GORDIE HOWE'S team records for assists and points in a season with a dozen games left to play. Dionne finishes with 47 goals, 74 assists, and 121 points, good for third place in the league scoring race. The Red Wings finish fourth in the five-team Norris Division, 14th in the 18-team league.

1975-76 MARCEL DIONNE MOVES TO THE LOS ANGELES KINGS. Detroit gets defenseman Terry Harper and winger Dan Maloney as compensation. Goalie Jim Rutherford ties a club record with three consecutive shutouts. Bruce Norris wins the Lester Patrick Trophy. The Red Wings stop Philadelphia's unbeaten streak at 23 games. Wings finish fourth in the Norris Division.

1976-77 BRYAN WATSON DRAWS A 10-GAME SUSPENSION for breaking Keith Magnuson's jaw. Watson is traded to Washington for Greg Joly. General manager Alex Delvecchio starts the season behind the Wings' bench, then gives way to Larry Wilson. Before the season is out, Delvecchio is also replaced as GM by Ted Lindsay. Detroit finishes dead last in the 18-team NHL, with only 16 wins and 41 points. They miss the playoffs for the seventh straight year, and the 10th time in 11 seasons.

1977-78 TED LINDSAY SENDS COACH LARRY WILSON to Oklahoma City, and hires Bobby Kromm to coach Detroit. With first choice overall in the draft, the Wings select Dale McCourt. Under Kromm the Wings improve to second place in the Norris Division with 78 points, get past Atlanta in the first round of the playoffs, then lose to Montreal in the quarterfinals. McCourt scores 33 goals as a rookie center. Kromm is named coach of the year.

1978-79 LONGTIME WING DEFENSEMAN Marcel Pronovost is inducted into the Hockey Hall of Fame. The Wings sign free agent goalie Rogie Vachon to a five-year deal, and lose Dale McCourt to the Kings as compensation. McCourt files a law suit in a successful attempt to block the deal. Gordie Howe plays for the WHA's New England Whalers against the Wings in an exhibition game. It's Howe's first time on Olympia ice since 1971. The Red Wings finish last in their division.

1979–80 DALE McCOURT WINS HIS FIGHT to stay in Detroit after having been negotiated as compensation for the Wings signing Rogie Vachon. Instead, Andre St. Laurent and two draft choices are sent to the Kings as compensation. Detroit hosts the NHL All-Star Game. The crowd of 21,002 at Joe Louis Arena is an All-Star record. On March 12, Gordie Howe and his sons play on a line for the Hartford Whalers against the Red Wings. Detroit finishes in last place in the Norris Division.

1980–81 DETROIT SENDS GOALIE ROGIE VACHON to Boston in return for goalie Gilles Gilbert. Ted Lindsay, fired by Detroit owner Bruce Norris, sues the team for $700,000 in back wages and severance pay. Wayne Maxner is hired as coach. The Wings finish 20th in the standings out of 21 teams.

1981–82 NICK POLANO IS HIRED AS COACH. League realignment leaves Detroit in the Norris Division, but with all-new rivals including the Minnesota North Stars, Winnipeg Jets, St. Louis Blues, Chicago, and Toronto. Detroit trades Dale McCourt, Mike Foligno, and Brent Peterson to Buffalo in return for Danny Gare, Derek Smith, and Jim Schoenfeld. Coach Wayne Maxner is fired and replaced by Billy Dea late in the season. Detroit finishes last in the new Norris Division and 20th overall for the second year in a row.

1982–83 A HALF CENTURY OF NORRIS FAMILY ownership ends when Mike Ilitch buys the Red Wings and two farm clubs for an estimated $9 million. Jimmy Devellano is hired to restructure the franchise. Former Red Wing Dennis Polonich receives an $850,000 settlement in his lawsuit against Wilf Paiement and the Colorado Rockies. Detroit finishes in last place in the Norris Division. They miss the playoffs for the fifth year in a row, and for the 15th time in 17 years.

1983–84 DETROIT SELECTS 18-YEAR-OLD Steve Yzerman in the entry draft. Brad Park is handed a two-year contract to play for Detroit. He wins the Bill Masterton Trophy for "perseverance, sportsmanship, and dedication to hockey." The Wings climb to third place in the Norris Division but are quickly eliminated by the St. Louis Blues in the first round of the playoffs. On November 25, a league-record 21,019 fans watch the Wings beat Pittsburgh 7–4.

1984–85 TIGER WILLIAMS IS ACQUIRED IN a trade with Vancouver. Later in the season he is dealt to Los Angeles. After the Wings are swept from the playoffs in the first round by Chicago, Brad Park announces his retirement.

1985–86 THE WINGS SIGN ADAM OATES, Ray Staszak, and other free agents to lucrative contracts. Staszak, after signing for $1.3 million, plays only four games for Detroit. Harry Neale is brought in to coach the Wings. Darryl Sittler, after one season as a Red Wing, retires. The Wings sign Petr Klima from Czechoslovakia, and predict he'll become a superstar. Harry Neale is fired after 35 games and replaced by Brad Park. Bruce Norris dies of liver failure. Detroit finishes last in the Norris Division. Their 40 points are the club's fewest since 1940, when they only played a 48-game schedule.

1986–87 BRAD PARK LOSES A BATTLE for control with Jimmy Devellano and is fired. He is replaced by Jacques Demers, lured away from St. Louis. The Wings draft Joe Murphy, a collegian from Michigan State, number one overall. Demers inspires his team to a second-place finish and a first-round win over Chicago in the playoffs. Demers is named coach of the year after his team is eliminated by Edmonton in the conference finals.

1987–88 THE RED WINGS REACH AN OUT-OF-COURT settlement with the Blues over the signing of coach Jacques Demers in 1986. Steve Yzerman scores his 50th goal against Buffalo. A few minutes later he sustains ligament damage to his knee. Detroit finishes on top of the Norris Division with 93 points and eliminates Toronto in the first round of the playoffs. Detroit also beats St. Louis to advance to the conference final, where Edmonton ousts them in five games. Demers wins his second straight Jack Adams Award as coach of the year.

1988–89 THE RED WINGS HAVE ONGOING problems involving alcohol and drug abuse by players Bob Probert and Petr Klima. Probert is expelled from hockey when a package containing cocaine falls out of his underwear on the U.S. side of the Detroit–Windsor tunnel. Steve Yzerman scores a team-record 65 goals. The Red Wings finish on top of the Norris Division with 80 points but lose to Chicago in the opening playoff round.

1989–90 THE RED WINGS TRADE PETR KLIMA, Adam Graves, Joe Murphy, and Jeff Sharples to Edmonton in return for Jimmy Carson, a 100-point scorer in 1988–89, Kevin McClelland, and a draft pick. Bob Probert makes a successful return to the Red Wing lineup after serving a year-long suspension for a drug conviction. Steve Yzerman scores 62 goals, but the Wings fall to last place in the Norris Division.

1990–91 THE RED WINGS SIGN SERGEI FEDOROV after the 20 year old defects from the Soviet team at the Goodwill Games. Brian Murray is hired as general manager and coach. Steve Yzerman tops 50 goals for the fourth straight season. The Red Wings bow out in the first round of the playoffs, losing to St. Louis in seven games. Red Wings owner Mike Ilitch wins the Lester Patrick Trophy.

1991–92 FOR THE SECOND TIME, STEVE YZERMAN is left off Team Canada's roster for the Canada Cup tournament. The Wings sign Sweden's Nicklas Lidstrom and Russian star Vladimir Konstantinov. Ted Lindsay and Alex Delvecchio have their jersey numbers retired (7 and 10). Detroit moves to the top of the Norris Division with 98 points. After trailing Minnesota 3–1 in games, the Wings come back to win their first-round play-off series in seven. The Blackhawks sweep the Red Wings aside in four games in the division finals.

1992–93 THE RED WINGS ACQUIRE SUPERSTAR defenseman Paul Coffey from the Kings for center Jimmy Carson. Steve Yzerman reaches the 1,000-point milestone. The Wings set team records for wins (47) and points (103) but still finish second in the Norris Division, three points behind Chicago. Toronto eliminates Detroit in seven games in the first playoff round.

1993–94 THE RED WINGS NAME SCOTTY BOWMAN as head coach, replacing Bryan Murray. Paul Coffey plays in his 1,000th career game and Scotty Bowman is credited with his 1,000th coaching win (including playoffs). The Wings win the Central Division (new name for the Norris Division) with 100 points, but fans call for Bowman's scalp after the Wings lose to the San Jose Sharks in the first playoff round. Ray Sheppard scores 52 goals. Sergei Fedorov wins both the Hart and the Selke Trophies.

1994–95 *FINANCIAL WORLD* MAGAZINE REPORTS

THE RED WINGS franchise is worth $104 million, tops in the NHL (Mike Ilitch paid an estimated $9 million for the troubled franchise in 1982). The Wings top the league with 33 wins and 70 points during the lock-out shortened season. The last time the team finished first overall was 1964–65. The Wings push the Dallas Stars aside in five games in the opening round of the play-offs, then oust San Jose and Chicago. In the Cup finals, the New Jersey Devils win the Stanley Cup in a four-game sweep of the Wings. Jim Devellano returns as GM, replacing Bryan Murray. Paul Coffey wins the Norris Trophy.

1995–96 ON DECEMBER 2, DETROIT HAMMERS

Montreal 11–1 at the Montreal Forum. Patrick Roy gives up nine of the goals and declares, "That's my last game as a Canadien." Scotty Bowman passes Al Arbour's record for games coached with 1,606. Former Detroit goalie Roger Crozier dies of prostate cancer. Steve Yzerman scores his 500th career goal. Red Wing goalie Chris Osgood scores an empty-net goal against Hartford. Osgood and Vernon win the Jennings Trophy with a league-leading lowest goals-against average. The Wings win a league-record 62 games and earn 131 points, also an all-time NHL high. The Wings eliminate the Winnipeg Jets and the St. Louis Blues in the first two rounds of the playoffs but lose to the Colorado Avalanche in six games in the Western Conference finals. Veteran center Igor Larionov is acquired from the San Jose Sharks for winger Ray Sheppard. The Wings win their second consecutive President's Trophy as first-place team overall. Sergei Fedorov wins his second Selke Trophy, and Scotty Bowman wins the Jack Adams Award.

1996–97 PAUL COFFEY, KEITH PRIMEAU, and a first-round draft choice are traded to Hartford in return for Brendan Shanahan and Brian Glynn. Shanahan scores a team-high 46 goals after the trade. Scotty Bowman registers his 1,000th regular-season coaching win. The Wings acquire defenseman Larry Murphy from Toronto. Detroit finishes on top of the Central Division with 38 wins and 94 points. In the playoffs, the Wings eliminate the Blues, the Anaheim Mighty Ducks, and the Avalanche to advance to the Cup finals. They stun Philadelphia with a four-game sweep to capture their first Cup in 42 years. Mike Vernon is named MVP of the series, and is awarded the Conn Smythe Trophy.

1997–98 THE RED WINGS FINISHED SECOND TO DALLAS in the Central Division and in third place overall, behind the Stars and the New Jersey Devils. Defenseman Nicklas Lidstrom led all NHL defensemen in scoring with 17 goals and 59 points. The Red Wings swept Washington in the Stanley Cup finals. Scotty Bowman earned his eighth Cup victory as a coach, tying him with Toe Blake for the all-time Cup record. Team captain Steve Yzerman won the Conn Smythe Trophy.